GEORGIAN
·SUMMER

GEORGIAN
·SUMMER·
The Rise and Development of Bath

DAVID GADD

COUNTRYSIDE BOOKS
NEWBURY BERKSHIRE

First Published by Moonraker Press 1971
Updated Edition 1987
© Estate of David Gadd 1987

COUNTRYSIDE BOOKS
3 Catherine Road
Newbury, Berkshire

ISBN 0 905392 60 4

Produced through MRM (Print Consultants) Ltd., Reading
Printed in England by Borcombe Printers Ltd., Romsey

CONTENTS

for Margaret

FOREWORD

This is the story of an extraordinary city and of the people who made it so. Bath is unique in England not only for the beauty of its Georgian buildings but for its history. A city which in 1700 was still medieval, provincial and insalubrious, became in less than a generation the hub of the fashionable world and within a hundred years could be compared with Florence. It is a fantastic climax to a story which began seventeen hundred years earlier with the building of the Roman baths.

A considerable literature has accumulated about Bath. Archaeologists and historians have studied its past; gossips and letter-writers like Horace Walpole and Chesterfield have given vivid accounts of the life of the fashionable visitor; since the seventeenth century physicians have advertised the merits of the spa with accounts of miraculous cures told in horrifying detail, thus obscuring the true virtues of the waters, which are only now being fully understood; amateur antiquaries have made valuable explorations of the historical byways; novelists like Smollett and Jane Austen, and playwrights like Sheridan have taken Bath as their scene.

Much of this literature is out of print—some of it was never in print at all—and hard to come by except in Bath itself, where the city library has a unique collection. The present work is based both on a study of this collection and on many days and miles on foot in the streets of Bath. It is meant, not for the specialist, but for the general reader with an interest in social history and a love of fine buildings. It claims to be historically accurate to the extent that it is ever sensible to make such a claim. It is indeed a serious book; but since much of it is concerned with the personalities and pursuits of a frivolous age, cheerfulness, in the words of Johnson's fellow-collegian, 'was alwasy breaking in' on the author as he wrote. Entertainment was the business of Bath: it would not be inappropriate if it were a by-product of a book about Bath.

I wish to express my warm gratitude to Mr Peter Pagan, BA, FLA, former Director of the City of Bath Libraries and Art Gallery, for his personal help and advice, and to his staff at Queen Square and the Victoria Art Gallery for their unfailing courtesy and helpfulness. Their knowledge was always at my disposal and they found sources and references for me with promptness and always with a smile. The list of Guildhall portraits which appears on page 186 was drawn up for me by Miss Jill Knight, Keeper of the Victoria Art Gallery: I am most grateful to her for this and other help.

Mr Terence Snailum, FRIBA, AA Dip Arch, the Bath architect and a good friend, made his expert knowledge generously available to me and was kind enough to show a friendly interest in the book as a whole. His criticism and encouragement were invaluable. Mr Michael Owen, late Curator of the Roman Baths, helped me greatly with comment and discussion about Bath in Roman times and the evidence provided by recent excavations.

I have also received assistance from Mr C. Storey, Dip TP, AMTPI, ex-Deputy Planning Officer of the City of Bath, and from Mr Hugh Crallan, FRIBA, late Hon. Secretary of the Bath Preservation Trust.

If, in spite of the help I have received from these and other sources, there are errors of fact or judgment, the fault is mine alone.

I have dedicated *Georgian Summer* to Margaret, who was very sweet about it for the four years during which it was my main preoccupation.

DAVID GADD

PREFACE TO NEW EDITION

My father was justly proud of *Georgian Summer* and was very eager to see this revised and updated edition published. Sadly, he died suddenly in March 1986 before it could take place.

My brother and I were born in Bath and have obvious personal affection for the city. This book therefore is particularly special to us as I know it was to my father.

We are delighted that it is now available again and hope that future readers will, like us, consider it a fitting memorial to his unfailing enthusiasm and love for this great city.

JENNY GADD

LIST OF ILLUSTRATIONS

The author and publisher are grateful for the help of the following in providing illustrations:

© Aldus Books *Gambling* by Alan Wykes, 1964, from a cartoon in the British Museum: 23; © J. Arthur Dixon Limited: 34; various departments of Bath City Council: frontispiece, 2, 3, 6, 7, 8, 9, 11, 14, 15, 18, 21, 22, 24, 25 (photograph by Miss Jane Bown of the *Observer*), 27, 30, 32, 33, 36, 37, 38, 40, 42, 45, 46, 47, 48, 49, 55, 57, 59, 61, and 26, 43, 44 and 50 (photographs by M. P. Wooller); *Bath Evening Chronicle*: 31; Bath Press Photo Services: 4, 13, 16, 19, 39; Bolwell Studio: 28, 35, 41, 51; V. C. Chamberlain: 20, 60; Darby Photographic Services: 1, 5; National Gallery of Art, Washington: 54; National Gallery, London: 53; National Portrait Gallery, London: 56; Post Office: 52; Alison and Peter Smithson, Architects: 58 and p. 69; Tate Gallery, London: 29; Victoria & Albert Museum: 10; E. J. Warren: 17.

Even now, after a century and a half of change, the heart of Bath has qualities of design that even the best examples in Paris, Nancy, London, or Edinburgh do not surpass.

LEWIS MUMFORD: The City in History

I

THE BACKGROUND

Bath is pre-eminently and for everyone the Georgian City, whose streets and buildings bring the eighteenth century to life as no other city does. It is a living record of the Age of Elegance. The splendour of its squares and crescents may well dazzle the visitor so that he hardly notices the absence of the medieval churches or Tudor mansions which are a feature of most of the ancient cities of England. It is almost as if Bath sprang into existence, in its full glory, in a few brief decades of architectural inspiration. The remains of earlier centuries do in fact exist, but they are few and are easily missed. The truth is that Bath was so completely rebuilt in the eighteenth century that most of the older city was demolished to make room for new buildings.

Only two buildings of major importance remain to indicate that Bath had a history before the days of Beau Nash: the Roman Baths and the Abbey church. Not only are they both of great intrinsic interest and merit, but each may stand as a vivid symbol of Bath's history. The background to the story of Georgian Bath may well therefore be written round these two memorials of the earlier life of the city.

First, however, it is proper to dispose of the story of the legendary founding of Bath by Prince Bladud—a strange name which no visitor to the city can avoid. The story exists in a number of forms, from the twelfth-century version of Geoffrey of Monmouth to the heavily embroidered accounts of later authors. Since legends are not strict history, a summary based on the

1

story as told by John Wood, the first great architect of Georgian Bath, is perhaps sufficient. The ancient British King, Lud Hudibras, had a son, Bladud, who suffered from a leprosy so vile that, although heir to the throne, he was forced to go into exile from his father's court. In his wanderings along the Avon he came to Cainsham (now Keynsham, situated between Bristol and Bath) where he became a swineherd. Like him, the pigs he tended were afflicted by a disease of the skin. One day Bladud with his swine came upon a steaming swamp by the river bank. His pigs at once plunged in and wallowed with every sign of ecstasy. When at last he got them to come out, he was astonished to see that their skins were quite healed. It was logical enough for Bladud to consider whether the hot mud would not also help his own case. He too plunged into the swamp and sure enough his leprosy vanished. He returned to his father's court, in due course became king, and in 863 BC (the legend gives the precise date) he established his seat at what is now Bath, building cisterns to retain the healing waters. It was here that he became the father of King Lear. The story is no more absurd than other legends. It has a kernel of truth in it, and was for centuries passionately believed in by the proud citizens of Bath.

We are on firmer ground with the arrival at Bath of the Romans. Their discovery and exploitation of the thermal springs gives Bath a history of nearly 2000 years. The discovery of the springs was, it is reasonable to assume, a happy accident. The Roman occupation of Britain had two main purposes: first to protect the flank of Gaul and secondly to provide access to the mineral wealth which the Phoenicians had been the first to exploit. Roman prospectors had, within a few years of the Claudian invasion in AD 43, found rich sources of silver-bearing lead in the Mendip Hills, a few miles west of Bath, and mines were quickly in operation—the mine-workings are still visible as tumbled grassy mounds near the villages of Priddy and Charterhouse. From the British labourers they employed, the Romans would soon have learned of the nearby hot springs, dedicated in

1 The Great Roman Bath
with the Abbey beyond

accordance with Celtic practice to a native goddess, Sul by name. Their reaction was immediate. Within fifty years they had built a bathing establishment, naming it *Aquae Sulis*, which was extended in the following century until it could rank with the great baths of Trier or Wiesbaden.

Roman Bath was extraordinary in more ways than one. First of all, it was simply and solely a spa. There is no evidence that it was ever a market town or administrative centre. It was certainly not a military headquarters; its site, a swampy patch of ground on a narrow un-navigable river closely surrounded by steep hills, rendered it quite without merit for such a function. For purposes of communication too it was valueless—a place any sensible Roman roadmaker would do everything possible to avoid. Nevertheless the Roman city throve, and was even provided eventually with a wall. Most surprising of all it became a major centre of road-communication in the province. The Fosse Way, the great strategic road from the Humber river to Exeter marking the boundary of the original Roman province, was forced into wildly untypical twists and turns to negotiate the Avon valley at the site of the city. Here it met the main road from London to Wales via the Severn crossing, and from here the road led off to Poole on the Dorset coast, a vital supply-route for the Roman colony. The fact is that the springs with their enormous and unfailing supply of naturally heated water provided more than enough reason for the rise of the Roman city. The present output of the springs is half-a-million gallons a day at a temperature of 48 degrees Centigrade; in Roman times the supply, though probably less than now, was adequate for the needs of a remarkable range of baths. These baths, whose existence was not suspected until the Great Bath was discovered and excavated in the 1880s, were among the largest in the Empire. The Great Bath, which originally had a vaulted roof, is over 80 feet long and still retains its floor of sheets of Mendip lead. There are plunge-baths and steam baths with smaller cold baths for use after the bather had been through the series of hot and tepid baths. There are mosaic pavements and hypocausts with their flues and hollow bricks. Beneath it all is a great reservoir with a culvert to carry away excess water. The whole establishment has now been uncovered suf-

2 Gorgon: barbaric centre-piece of temple pediment, Aquae Sulis

ficiently for the visitor to gain a true impression of the size and splendour of its original form.

Like the British the Romans too invested springs and rivers with tutelar deities, wherever possible identifying the native god or goddess with a member of the Roman pantheon. In this case, appropriately enough, they identified the British goddess Sul with Minerva the Roman goddess of healing, and there are a number of votive tablets dedicated to Sul-Minerva to be seen in the Roman Baths Museum. Not only was a temple erected in her honour, but it was built, not in the primitive native style deemed adequate for similar sanctuaries throughout the Empire, but in the true metropolitan style of Rome itself. It now lies hidden under Stall Street with the forecourt partly beneath the Pump Room. Excavations carried out in 1963–65 have however established all its main features and have revealed a building resembling closely the Maison Carrée at Nîmes, one of the best-preserved Roman temples outside Italy. It was surrounded by a wide precinct, with a sacrificial altar located under the north wall of the Pump Room. The pediment of the temple has been partially reassembled from excavated fragments, and is set up in the museum. Its centre-piece is a magnificent barbaric head,

5

3 Minerva: classical bronze from
the Baths, found in 1727

clearly the work of a British craftsman. It is generally described
as a Gorgon's Head, and the artist has certainly been influenced
by that popular design with its snake-locks and malignant expression. The face, however, is not that of a Medusa. It is a fearsome
male bearded figure with wild hair and clear traces of wings on
either side of the face. It is strange that such a figure should have
the place of honour in the temple of a goddess. Does it perhaps
represent some lost British Jove, Father of the Gods?

Whatever doubt there may be about this great head, there is
none about the equally splendid bronze-gilt head of Minerva,
unearthed in 1727. Complete except for its helmet, it is of excellent classical design, and though doubtless of provincial work-
manship, impeccably Roman. It forms a striking contrast with
the bearded Gorgon, and the two heads may be taken to sym-
bolise the co-existence of native and Roman culture in the
provinces of the Empire.

None of the other buildings of Aquae Sulis, which lie up to
fifteen feet below the streets of modern Bath, has been fully
excavated, but we know that they were few, and that the whole
area of the city was little more than twenty acres in extent. The
medieval walls, which seem to have followed the line of the

Roman wall, ran from what is now Bridge Street along Upper Borough Walls (where a few yards of the wall are still standing) to the Sawclose, then south-east along Westgate Buildings and Lower Borough Walls, to rejoin Bridge Street via North Parade and the Orange Grove.

From the inscriptions on tombstones and votive tablets we know that the Roman spa drew its visitors not only from the

4 The medieval city wall: section still standing in Upper Borough Walls

Roman forces and colonists in Britain but also from north-west Europe. In short, the evidence provided by the scale of the buildings and the number and style of inscriptions leaves no doubt that Aquae Sulis was among the great medicinal spas of the Roman world.

After three-and-a-half centuries of turbulent rule, the Romans left and never returned. The fairly clear picture we have of Roman Bath fades and for centuries there are only scattered hints of its history. We know that it was one of the cities to fall to the invading Saxons in the sixth century. Two hundred years later, lines in a Saxon poem probably refer to Bath:

There stood arcades of stone: the stream hotly issued, with eddies widening up to the wall encircling all the bright bosomed pool; there the baths were—hot with inward heat. . . . Wondrous the wall-stone that Weird [i.e. fate] hath broken. The roof-tree riven, the grey gates despoiled. . . . The stone court stands and the hot stream hath whelmed it, there where the bath was hot on the breast.

This extract gives a plausible picture of the fate of the city, with its buildings fallen into ruin in the absence of Roman maintenance, and the site slowly reverting to swamp.

When at last Bath emerged from the mists of the Dark Ages, it was to embark on a new historical career, which would culminate in the building of the Abbey church, the second great symbol of pre-eighteenth-century Bath. In the seventh century the Abbess Bertana was given a grant of land for a nunnery 'near the city called Hat Bathu' and in the following year Offa, King of Mercia, built a minster at Bath. For the next 800 years Bath was first and foremost an ecclesiastical centre. Its importance can be measured by the fact that Edgar, the first king of all England, was crowned at Bath in AD 973, and it was Edgar who brought to the city the Benedictine monks. Their successors ruled the city for over 500 years. Their last great work was the building of the Abbey church we now see.

Massively destroyed in the civil strife following the death of William the Conqueror, Bath was bought, for the sum of £60, by John de Villula, also known as John of Tours, who was at the same time a court physician and Bishop of Somersetshire. He also acquired the Abbey and built himself a new palace at Bath, which he chose as his seat instead of Wells. As a physician, the bishop fostered the treatment of the sick poor in the hospitals which already existed in the city (St John's Hospital, the oldest remaining City Charity, was founded shortly after his death in 1174). His most notable work was the building of a new church for the Abbey. Over a hundred yards long, the great Norman church stood on the site of the present Abbey and extended over much of the Orange Grove. Its scale is indicated by the fact that the present Abbey covers only the site of the Norman nave. An arch at the east end of the Abbey and a little stonework are all that remain of the twelfth-century church.

Since the city had become ecclesiastical property the baths were also controlled by the Church. A new bath was constructed for the use of the bishop's royal guests and it is to this fact that the present King's Bath owes its name. For the rest it was the poor who mainly benefited from the waters. The monks regarded the hot springs as a gift of God and applied them to charitable purposes, not to commercial ends.

The *Gesta Stephani* of 1138 mentions the baths. It refers to

streamlets of water, warmed without human agency, and from the very bowels of the earth, into a receptacle beautifully constructed, with chambered arches. These form baths in the middle of the city, warm and wholesome, and charming to the eye. Sick persons from all over England resort thither to bathe in these healing waters, and the fit also, to see these wonderful burstings out of warm water and to bathe in them.

Already, it seems, the medicinal value of the waters had more than a local reputation. The first reference to their efficacy as a cure for leprosy—a generic name applied to any stubborn skin disease—occurs in 1250 and later references are frequent. Already, too, tourists had apparently begun to visit Bath.

The monks were, it seems, not greatly interested in the baths and did nothing to improve their facilities. They had other pre-occupations. There was, for example, the long wrangle with the secular Canons of Wells as to who should elect the bishop, a wrangle settled in the end by a statesmanlike edict from the Holy See, which gave the diocese its present name of Bath *and* Wells. The bishop was to be jointly elected, but his seat was moved to

Wells, where the present splendid palace was built by Bishop Jocelyn in the thirteenth century.

When there were no exciting controversies of this kind to divert their attention, the monks were busy enough with their duties not only as a religious body but as landowners. They became the main and indeed virtually the only employers of labour in the city. The wool industry which gave the city its livelihood was under their control, and it was they who introduced the craft of weaving in the fourteenth century, adding a weaver's shuttle to the arms of the Abbey to mark the fact. Chaucer's Wife of Bath, it will be remembered, was a weaver, so skilful in cloth-making that she 'passed them of Ypres and of Ghent'. The Black Death of 1349 reduced the numbers of monks to some twenty and the monastery never regained its former strength. A period of lethargy and neglect ensued, and by the following century the Abbey church itself had fallen into ruin.

Towards the end of the fifteenth century, Bishop Oliver King set himself the task both of restoring the discipline of the monks and of rebuilding the church. How successful he was as a reformer is doubtful—though the scandalous report[1] of Thomas Cromwell's agent at the time of the Dissolution is certainly a libel—but Bath Abbey stands as evidence of his ability as a builder.

The bishop's decision to rebuild the church was the result, it is said, of a dream in which he heard a voice say 'Let an Olive establish the crown and a King restore the Church'. He interpreted this as a divine order that he, Oliver, should support the Tudor cause (then much in need of such backing) and that he, King, should rebuild the Abbey. The interpretation hardly flatters the Almighty: the play on words is deplorable enough by

5 Abbey west front, with Pump Room on right

---

[1] The report includes such statements as the following:

The Prior a right virtuous man . . .; his monks worse than I have any found yet in buggery and adultery, some of them having ten women, some eight and the rest fewer. (Quoted by R. A. L. Smith in *Bath*.)

human standards. The bishop however did as he thought he had been told. To commemorate his dream, an olive tree supporting a crown and surmounted by a mitre adorns the pillars at each end of the west front. Angels mounting and descending ladders on the same front provide a charming touch of fantasy.

The new Abbey church, appropriately called the Lantern of England because of the huge expanse of windows lighting the nave, was the last great church to be built before the break with Rome. It was also the first English church for which fan-vaulting was included in the original plans. Building began in 1499 and continued after the bishop's death, under Prior Birde and his successors, until it was brought to a halt at the Dissolution of the monasteries in 1539. All the monastic buildings were then sold and demolished. The dormitory, refectory and cloister fetched £24, while the bells went for £98. The library was pillaged by Cromwell. Only the Abbey church, still roofless and unglazed, and the Prior's Lodging on its south side remained. The church was offered to the city for use as a parish church for 500 marks, but was refused: there were already five such churches in Bath, and that was enough. Bought by Edmund Colthurst, Member of Parliament for Bath, it was later presented by him to the city, after the north aisle had been made fit for use by private initiative.

In 1574 Queen Elizabeth visited Bath on a progress through the western counties. She was so shocked by the ruinous state of the church that she sponsored a nation-wide fund for its restoration. She also ordered the consolidation of the many Bath parishes into one, with the Abbey, as soon as it was restored, as the parish church. It is for this reason that Bath has no medieval church: having no income after the consolidation of parishes, they fell into ruin and were ultimately demolished. Only St Mary Magdalene at Holloway, which was outside the medieval city, still has a fifteenth-century nave. The restoration of the Abbey took many years. Although the nave was in use within a short time, it was not roofed until the next century, by the generosity

6 The Abbey: the nave looking west

of Bishop Montague, whose disproportionately large tomb stands in the nave today. This first roof of lath and plaster was not replaced by stone vaulting until the nineteenth century.

On the whole, time and the restorers have dealt kindly with the Abbey. Its nave and choir, with no intervening screen, provide a lovely vista of vaults and piers in the clear light of the great nave windows. It has its place among the great churches of England. Besides being a building of high intrinsic merit, the Abbey serves as a link—almost the only link—between the city of Doomsday times and the fashionable spa of the eighteenth century. The square-headed east window is so shaped to conform with the roof of the Norman church it replaced. The walls, in which much of the stone of the old church was re-used, are thronged with memorials to the famous and obscure who came to Georgian Bath for healing, and came in vain. An irreverent verse of the time recorded:

> These walls, so full of monument and bust,
> Shew how Bath waters serve to lay, the dust.

The disappearance of Bath as an ecclesiastical centre at the Dissolution coincided with a serious decline in the weaving industry. It was fortunate that for some time the baths had been attracting more and more visitors, and by the sixteenth century it is true to say that they constituted the city's main source of income. Thus, after a gap of more than a thousand years, Bath became once more what it was under the Romans—a spa, and nothing but a spa. It is as if, in the intervening centuries, Bath had lost its way in history: now it assumed once more its true rôle. Henceforward it is only as a watering-place that Bath claims our interest.

The two baths belonging to the monastery disappeared before the Dissolution and Leland in his *Itinerary*, covering his journey through England in the years 1534–43, refers to three only: he noted that the Cross Bath was 'much frequentid of people diseas'd with lepre, pokkes, scabbes and great aches, and is temperate and pleasant, having 11. or 12. arches of stone in the sides for men to stonde under yn tyme of reyne'. The Hot Bath had only seven arches, he recorded, while the fair and large King's Bath was 'cumpassid with an high stone waulle. . . . In

14

this waul be 32. arches for men and women to stand separately yn.'

In 1554, the baths came under the control of the city for the first time. Although still regarded primarily as an amenity for the free use of the poor, they were now also seen as a valuable capital asset capable of bringing wealth to the town. Distinguished physicians were beginning to publicise the medicinal virtue of the waters. In 1538 William Turner, the 'master of English physicke', included in his 'Herball' a laudatory section on the 'Bath of Baeth in England', and this was quoted in *The Englishman's Treasure*, a popular work in high favour at the time. In 1572 John Jones, 'Gent., Graduate in Physicke', wrote:

The Bathes of Bathes Ayde, wonderful and most excellent, agaynst very many sicknesses, approved by authoritie, confirmed by reason, and dayly tried by experience.

He also recommended the drinking of the waters, and may thus be considered to have laid the foundation-stone of the Pump Room. Soon after his book appeared a drinking fountain was

7 The King's Bath emptied, showing seats and rings

15

installed at the King's Bath. As a result of these and other writings, the stream of wealthy invalids grew steadily. At the same time a small army of doctors, many of them quacks, set up in practice at Bath, often adding to their income by lodging patients in their own homes. Although there were more than a dozen inns they were crowded, uncomfortable and always dirty.

The city fathers decided at about this time to appoint a small staff to maintain the baths and to assist the bathers. This consisted of a Sergeant who supervised the whole establishment and paid the city an annual fee of forty shillings for the privilege, and a number of Guides who attended the bathers and cleaned the baths. They received payment from the city for operating the newly installed Dry Pump, designed to direct a stream of water onto a specific part of the body, but otherwise depended on gratuities. The Cross Bath and the Hot Bath were emptied and cleaned daily, but the King's Bath only twice a week. As the number of bathers grew this was patently inadequate.

To cope with the increasing crowds of bathers, the city decided to build

a convenyent newe Bath adioyninge to the said King's Bath ... which shall serve for women severallie from the King's Bath there, and in the absence of women men to have resort thyther in such order as the Mayor and justyces of the sayd cytye or ther officers shall appoint.

The new bath was in use by 1576, but had no particular name until the following century, when it became known as the Queen's Bath. John Wood tells how it gained the name. His story is that Anne of Denmark, James I's queen, who made two visits to Bath in search of a cure for dropsy, was one day bathing in the King's Bath when a sudden flame shot up from the water and spread over the surface. Frightened out of her royal wits, she moved quickly to the adjacent 'New Bath' which she henceforth used exclusively.

Apart from the Queen's Bath, only minor improvements were undertaken in the following years by the cautious Common Council of the city. An attempt to provide a roof for the Hot Bath failed, and was not made a second time. A small bath, measuring only twelve feet square, was provided for the use of poor persons suffering from skin ailments. This bath, the Lepers' Bath, no longer exists. Another, made at this time, has also disappeared. This was the Horse Bath on the banks of the river, fed by surplus water from the King's Bath, where the animals for whom it was constructed could rid themselves of mire from the wretched roads leading to the city.

It was at this time that the beggars of Bath became a byword. As an act of charity parish authorities frequently sent their sick poor to spas like Bath or Buxton at the expense of the parish. At Bath an increasing number of the recipients of this form of charity tended to stay on after their 'cure', thus establishing residence and the right to poor relief at their new home. A growing number of towns seized on this convenient method of getting rid of their unwanted paupers. Once settled at Bath, these wretched creatures lived by begging from the wealthy patrons of the spa. Here they were in competition with the professional beggars, a great horde of whom, camping in squalor at Holloway, just outside the city's jurisdiction, thronged the streets and importuned visitors and citizens alike.

The scandal became so great that two sixteenth-century Acts of Parliament, designed to control vagrancy, specifically mentioned Bath:

The inhabitants of the same Citie [viz. Bath] . . . shall not in any wyse bee charged by this Acte with the fyndinge or relief of any such poore people.

Unfortunately one of the Acts confirmed the right of the diseased poor to the free use of the baths and although this Act was later repealed, the damage was done. The Beggars of Bath were established as a recognised social category and 'Go to Bath' was a common phrase used to dismiss importunate beggars anywhere in England.

The city authorities had other problems. One of them was the time-honoured practice of nude mixed bathing, which they tried in vain to stop, even enlisting the august aid of the Privy Council for the purpose. A report of as late as 1634 remarks that the bathers appearing 'so nakedly and fearfully, in their uncouth naked postures, would a little astonish and putt one in mind of the Resurrection'. Johnson's well-known drawing of the King's

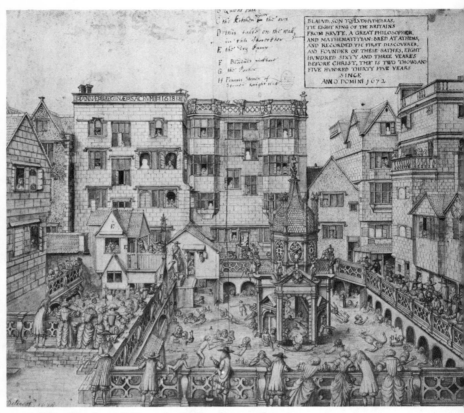

8 The King's and Queen's Baths, from a drawing
by Thomas Johnson, 1675 (Pump Room)

and Queen's Baths in 1675[8] confirms the practice, and John Wood writing of this period, makes his disapproval clear:

The baths were . . . like so many bear-gardens, and modesty entirely shut out of them, people bathing by night and day stark naked.

Not all the patrons of the baths were as censorious. Samuel Pepys, who paid a visit in 1668, had doubts about the hygiene of mass bathing. 'Methinks,' he wrote in his Diary, 'It cannot be clean to go so many bodies together in the same water.' He had however no other complaint to make. Although it was four

18

o'clock in the morning when he went to the Cross Bath, he was sufficiently awake to enjoy the sight of the 'very fine ladies' bathing with him.

At the time of Pepys' visit Bath was still essentially a small medieval city of no more than 250 houses and a population of less than twelve hundred. It was still largely confined within its ancient walls. Only the weavers had settled in what is now Broad Street, drying their wool on racks set up where Milsom Street now stands. In 1622 the Mayor complained that 'we are a verie little poore Citie, our Clothmen much decayed and many of their workmene amongst us relieved by the Citie'. It is true that the failure of the weaving industry was irretrievable; but the 'little poore Citie', with its decaying houses cramped together in narrow dirty streets, was on the verge of fame and wealth.

There can be no doubt that it was royal patronage which transformed Bath from a watering-place not vastly superior to Buxton or Harrogate into the unique resort of the fashionable world it was to become. The visits of Anne of Denmark were followed in 1677 by the arrival of Charles II, who brought with him his queen, Catherine of Braganza, in the vain hope that a course of the waters would enable her to produce an heir to the throne. He seems to have enjoyed his stay enough to make later visits, accompanied on these occasions not by the Queen but once by the Duchess of Cleveland (better known by her earlier title of Lady Castlemaine) and once by Louise de Kéroualle, successively his mistresses. The precise aim of these visits is not known; certainly the ladies did not suffer from barrenness. The Duchess provided a ring for the wall of the King's Bath, inscribed with the royal arms bearing a bar sinister. In 1687 James II visited Bath with Mary of Modena, his second wife. In the following year, and again four years later, his daughter Princess Anne, who suffered from gout, came to take the waters, accompanied by her husband, Prince George of Denmark. In 1702, the year in which she became queen, she made a third visit and a fourth in the following year.

The royal visitors were accommodated in the Abbey House, formerly the Prior's Lodging, which was reserved for distinguished visitors. They were luckier than the courtiers in their train, who had to make do with what the inns and private lodgings could provide. Four visits by the reigning monarch were a clear mark of favour, and court circles were quick to follow the Queen's lead. 'Everyone', said Swift a few years later, 'is going to Bath.' So indeed they were, to the mixed delight and embarrassment of its citizens. The sudden descent of noble and wealthy visitors in holiday mood could not have been more welcome to the inn-keepers and tradesmen, but the city authorities knew only too well that Bath was ill-equipped to provide the amenities expected by its new patrons.

The streets were unpaved and unlit and infested with pickpockets. Beggars, as we have seen, abounded. Quacks and cardsharpers competed with each other to rob the visitors. The sedan chairmen bullied and insulted their passengers. Lodgings were still dingy and too few.

Facilities for entertainment were equally inadequate. For the physically energetic there were two tennis courts and two bowling greens. There were occasional dances at the Guildhall, and there were one or two fly-blown coffee-houses. Sherry could be taken at the Bristol milk dairy and it is said, not very credibly, that there was good wine and company to be had at an inn known as Horrid Tom's. Gaming was of course readily available, but there was little for those who preferred an alternative. At infrequent intervals travelling companies performed at the Guildhall or in inn courtyards. In this connection it is interesting to speculate whether Shakespeare was a member of Burbage's company when it played at Bath at the beginning of the century. Shakespeare would certainly have been familiar with the reputation of Bath and two of his sonnets (Nos. CLIII and CLIV) refer to hot springs which he may well himself have visited there.[1]

In the face of every inconvenience and inadequacy however

---

[1] Part of the latter sonnet reads:

> *This brand she quenched in a cool well by*
> *Which from Love's fire took heat perpetual,*
> *Growing a bath and healthful remedy*
> *For men diseased; but I, my mistress' thrall,*
> *Came there for cure, and this by that I prove,*
> *Love's fire heats water, water cools hot love.*

the number of visitors continued to rise. In this situation the lethargy of the city authorities was remarkable. They did practically nothing to improve the standard or scope of the amenities available. It is true that by the beginning of the eighteenth century the scandal of nude bathing had at last been removed. No other concessions had been made to the refined tastes of the new clientele, except that a Master of Ceremonies had now been appointed. He might have done much to improve the standard of entertainment if he had spent less time at the gaming tables.

Finding themselves in a setting whose canons were so different from court or the great houses to which they were accustomed, the visitors adjusted their behaviour accordingly. They dressed as they pleased without regard to normal rules of propriety, they sat up all night gaming, they quarrelled with each other at rowdy drinking parties, they snubbed or insulted their social inferiors. Life for the citizens was profitable enough, but must have been in every other way well-nigh intolerable.

While the tradesmen were content to accept their sudden good fortune and let the future look after itself, there were others— speculators, physicians and other leaders of the community— who were beginning to have a hazy vision of what Bath might become. What was lacking was the initiative, energy and expertise required to turn the vision into reality.

9 (*overleaf*) The City of Bath, 1692, from the survey by Joseph Gilmore

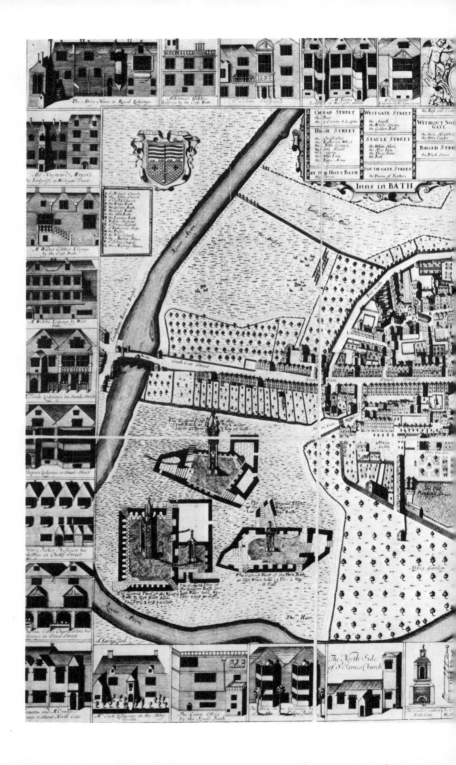

The Abby House to Royal Lodgings

Al. Kaman Gibbes Lodging by the Cross Bath

S. Johns Hospitall

Lodging in West gate Street

Mr. Chesterlaine

Ald. Hayward (Mayor) his Lodgings in West gate Street

Mr. Walter Gibbes Lodgings by the Cross Bath

Mr. Webb Lodgings by West Gate

Mr. Forde Lodgings in Staule Street

Mr. Slopers Lodgings in Staule Street

Henry Parker his Session his Lodgings in Cheap Street

John Gibbs Chamberlaine his Lodgings in Staule Street

Deacons and Mr Crookes his Lodgings without North Gate

Mr Cales Lodgings in the Abby Green

The Cann Office by the Kings Bath

The three Tuns Lodgings by the Kings Bath

River Arm

River Arm

Corsham Road to Bristol

South Gate Street

South Gate

Staule Street

North Gate

Abby Green

Abby Garden

Abby Garden

The North Side of S James Church

Inns in BATH

River Arm

The Ham

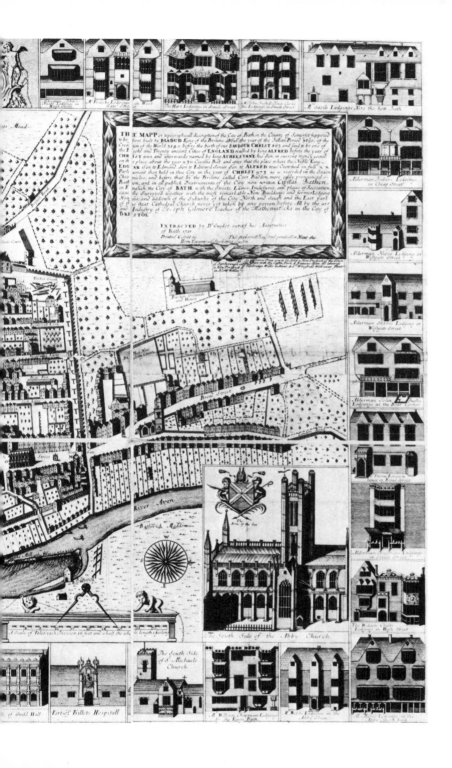

II

EIGHTEENTH-CENTURY BATH: THE ORIGINS

Thus, as the new century opened, Bath stood without knowing it at the parting of the ways. On the one hand the mode could change overnight and the fashionable crowds depart as suddenly as they had come. For the bulk of the tradesmen, content to take a quick profit, this seemed perhaps the most likely prospect. There was however the barely considered possibility of consolidating the new fame of the city from an ephemeral whim of fashion into a durable reputation. Characteristically the city fathers were not ready to invest much money on improvements which might never show a return. Neither the Corporation nor the men of business were in any case sufficiently familiar with the tastes and requirements of the fashionable world to know what improvements were likely to make the most appeal. A few timid projects were considered but little was done to realise them. Left to themselves it seems certain that the citizens of Bath would have let fortune slip through their fingers. Soon enough the discomforts of a provincial watering-place would have driven the elegant crowds away. The fact that this did not occur was due both to luck and to the vision and energy of three men—Richard 'Beau' Nash, Ralph Allen and John Wood: a gambler, a wealthy businessman and an architect.

The element of luck consisted in Nash's decision to leave London and try his fortune in Bath. In taking this step he was merely joining the stream of gamblers and card-sharpers, professionals like himself, who realised the opportunity presented there by moneyed visitors with time on their hands. Nash had not always been a gambler by trade. An educated man, he had made an unsatisfactory start in more than one career, and in the process had acquired the tastes and manners of London society. In 1705 when he arrived in Bath he was twenty-nine years old. His success as a gambler depended not upon skill at cheating—he usually seems to have played fair—but on a combination of intelligent play and personality. He was an entertaining companion to whom it was a pleasure to lose. His impact on Bath was immediate and striking. He was at once taken up both by the visitors and by Captain Webster, the Master of Ceremonies. Webster was an uncouth figure, addicted to cards and drink. When, shortly after Nash's arrival, he was killed in a duel over a gambling dispute Nash was his obvious successor, thus inheriting the title of King of Bath, borne *ex officio* by the Master of Ceremonies. In a short time he was to give real meaning to what for his predecessor had been an empty honorific.

Nash had already acquired a certain reputation as a social organiser and he seized with enthusiasm this new opportunity to enhance it. Gifted with what Goldsmith called an 'impenetrable assurance', he was at the same time a charmer, a dandy, an adventurer and an insolent, frivolous and conceited snob, with a kind heart and a fortune still to make. A superficial, trivial creature, with a strong taste for all the gentlemanly vices of the age, he had one saving grace—a passion for order and propriety. And what he saw at Bath horrified him. Sharing to the full the tastes of the fashionable visitors, he had exactly the talents and the determination needed to put right what was wrong in the rapidly developing life of the city. He had too the boldness required to impose the reforms he saw to be necessary.

It is easy to sneer at Nash; his faults are obvious enough and it is fair to say that his gifts were on the whole slight, or at least that they were devoted to slight ends. But the extraordinary fact is that what he achieved at Bath by way of the regulation of society was in due course to affect the country at large and to affect it for the good. In the sober words of Trevelyan, the social historian, 'Nash did perhaps as much as any other person even in the eighteenth century to civilise the neglected manners of mankind.' In any list of men whose work has had a dramatic and permanent effect on the development of English life, Nash's name must have its place.

His love for order, decency and cleanliness, rare enough at the time, amounted to an obsession, and this obsession was to be his driving force as Master of Ceremonies. His official powers were indeed tenuous; he was king only by the consent, which could at any time be brutally withdrawn, of those over whom he ruled. Nevertheless his personal authority soon amounted to a dictatorship, at times resented, often laughed at, but always in the end accepted.

Immediately on his appointment, Nash set about a massive cleaning-up operation both in the physical and social spheres. First, he insisted with the Corporation that the streets should be properly cleaned and even paved, and that the lodgings should not only be improved but submitted to regular inspection. Since the roads on the approaches to Bath were in a dangerous state of neglect, he raised private subscriptions amounting to nearly £2000 for their repair, thus showing a genius as a fund-raiser which was one of his greatest gifts. He then turned a baleful eye on the sedan chairmen, an unruly set of rogues, who had the monopoly of public transport in the city and whose tyrannical treatment of their fares had long been a scandal. Celia Fiennes, writing in 1690 of a visit to Bath, had said

There are chairs as in London to carry the better sort of people, but no control is exercised over them; they imposed what fares they chose and when these were disputed would not let their customers go. If it was raining they would open the top and let him or her, often an invalid, be exposed to the wet until in despair the charges were met.

By Nash's insistence the chairmen were brought under a degree of control by the issue of licences (limited at first to sixty) and the regulation of fares. The sedan chair, called officially a Glass chair or Bath chair, was to be in general use at Bath until the nineteenth century when the roads were paved. Then the wheeled Bath chair came into vogue for the transport of invalids, and horse-drawn carriages served the healthy. Accompanied at night by link-boys carrying torches, the sedan chairmen took their fares, wherever possible, into their houses and delivered them at the door of their lodging. On several houses in the city link-extinguishers shaped like outsize candle-snuffers still stand at the front door, and many houses built at the time have unusually spacious rounded landings to enable sedan chairs to be easily turned after depositing their passengers.

There was, when Nash arrived, no provision for the indoor entertainment of the visitor, no theatre, no concert hall and no place of assembly in bad weather. Nash at once set to work to get buildings provided. Meanwhile he did what he could out-doors. The Gravel Walks, the present Orange Grove, formerly a squalid and unseemly area, had been newly laid out with paths and planted with trees. A terrace of houses was being built on the south side and here, on Nash's insistence, 'a handsome pavement was then made for the company to walk on'. As time went on, wide pavements of this kind were to be characteristic of John Wood's Bath.

*　　*　　*

For some time the doctors of Bath had been pressing for a Pump Room to be built where their patients could drink the waters in comfort. At the head of the physicians in their campaign was the renowned Dr William Oliver, whose name is perpetuated in the Bath Oliver, a biscuit still made to the recipe he devised to suit the low diet of those taking a course of the waters. Nash brought the full force of his personality into the battle, and the Corporation hurriedly gave in. Funds were raised and in 1706 the first Pump Room was built. It stood on the site of the present building though it was only half its size. Nevertheless it was a start and Nash was as pleased as the doctors. Some of the London physicians however were less pleased, rightly fearing the competition of the provincial spa. Dr John Radcliffe, Queen Anne's Court Physician, was particularly incensed at what he saw as a challenge to the pre-eminence of the metropolitan doctors. Pouring scorn on the efficacy of Bath waters, he threatened to poison them by casting toads into the spring. Nash's reaction was characteristic and effective. He hired a band

10 The Lower Rooms (Harrison's) with Lindsey's Rooms
(built by John Wood the Elder in 1728) to the left of
picture, from a drawing for an aquatint by Thomas Malton,
c. 1777

of six musicians to play daily in the Pump Room and announced

I will fiddle the amphibious creatures out of the hot waters: and, by
the power of harmony, charm every one on whom the toad should spit
his poison into such a dance as should drive out the venom and turn
languishment itself into gaiety.

Nash's fiddlers represented the first attempt to provide music for
the visitors, who paid a subscription of a guinea for the amenity.
Nash learned that Thomas Harrison, a local man, had in mind
the building of an Assembly House as a speculative venture.
Persuaded by Nash, he went ahead with the project and by 1708
the building was complete and ready for use. It stood between
the Terrace Walk and the river, overlooking Harrison's Walks,
which had been laid out by the same developer, and was a

popular place of promenade. Consisting at first only of a card-room and tea-rooms, it was an immediate success, and a ballroom was added in 1720.

Harrison's Rooms became the social hub of Bath, and Nash moved his small orchestra there from the Pump Room. From these small beginnings grew the regular Assembly Room Concerts which have been a feature of Bath life for 250 years.

Having contrived a framework within which social life could develop on agreeable lines, Nash turned a basilisk eye on the visitors themselves. He was not pleased with what he saw. The dress, manners and general deportment of Bath society fell far below the standard he regarded as acceptable. He acted with boldness. A rapid fire of instructions and exhortations, more remarkable for their pungency of language than for their delicacy of phrasing, came from both the tongue and the pen of the Master of Ceremonies. Informal dress, and in particular riding boots and aprons, were banned from public assemblies. Gambling was brought under a degree of control. He forbade duelling and even the wearing of swords in the city. He insisted that balls should end on the stroke of eleven. He issued a code of rules to cover the less clear-cut aspects of social demeanour. Ignorance would no longer be an excuse for offences against the usages of polite society. The London aristocracy who thought they could forget, as long as they were staying at a small West Country spa, the formalities which were *de rigueur* in Town, were rapidly disillusioned. The strange thing is that the majority of visitors, however high their rank, accepted the rules laid down by Nash, and generally with a good grace. The result was an orderly, even a regimented, way of life and a code of behaviour which, though too rigid by modern standards, at least eliminated the vulgarity and coarseness characteristic of the time.

Seven years after Nash's arrival in Bath, Ralph Allen, an eighteen-year-old Cornishman, took up the post of Deputy Postmaster in the same city. The grandson of the postmistress at St Columb in Cornwall, he was a youth of obvious ability, character and ambition. The postal service was at this time farmed out to contractors. These in their turn appointed local postmasters, one of whose main tasks was to sort the mail and arrange its delivery to the smaller towns and villages not served by the direct posts. Allen found a scandalous situation. The postmasters either pocketed the fees for such local letters without delivering them, or else demanded a fee on delivery which again was kept by the postmaster. Either way the Revenue was defrauded. The inspections carried out by Allen revealed that the loss to public funds was huge. He saw that under proper supervision the service could be greatly improved and the Post Office's revenue raised; what he lacked was the capital necessary to purchase the concession to operate the posts. He had however a friend to whom he was able to turn. In 1715 he had got wind of a supply of arms on its way to the Jacobite rebels in the West of England. He alerted General Wade, whose headquarters were at Bath, who was not only grateful for the information, but was struck by the personality and gifts of the informant. He used his influence to get Allen appointed chief postmaster at Bath and soon after was happy to assent to Allen's marriage to his natural daughter. When Allen was ready to bid for a share of the control of the postal service he was one of those who guaranteed him the financial support he required. With this backing, Allen was able to offer £6000 a year for the right to operate the Bye Way and Cross-road postal service, that is, the delivery of letters to places not served by the main routes. In return he undertook to raise the revenue from this source by £2000 a year, any profit above that figure, if any, being his. In spite of opposition from local postmasters who saw their opportunities to defraud the Post Office threatened by the intrusion of this knowledgeable and sharp-eyed newcomer, and the absurd conditions proposed by ignorant financial advisers to the Postmasters General, Allen finally got his agreement on terms acceptable to him. He set about the effective transformation of the 'cross posts', as the service for which he was now responsible was loosely called. By a system of thorough and regular inspection he soon identified and dismissed the worst of the fraudulent postmasters. He then introduced his own methods to ensure an efficient service and to prevent further fraud. Not only did he reveal the administrative genius that was to take him to great heights later, but he showed that he could handle men. The very postmasters whose efforts to

11 Ralph Allen, by Thomas Hudson, 1754

cheat the Revenue were frustrated by his alertness, and who were not infrequently called to his office to be thoroughly dressed down, became in due course his most loyal supporters. Allen had made an excellent bargain, and so had the Post Office. In the course of increasing both the efficiency and the profitability of the 'cross posts', he made a fortune.

He now had the capital with which to consider new activities. The rage for building in the classical style, inspired by Burlington and Colin Campbell, was now at its height. The demand for suitable stone was enormous, particularly in London, which had no nearby sources of its own. Allen bought the stone quarries at Combe Down on the outskirts of Bath, hoping not only to supply the city's needs, which he foresaw to be considerable, but to obtain a share of the London market. The Avon had recently been made commercially navigable as far up-river as Bath, and it was thus possible to ship stone to any part of the country by sea. Unfortunately Bath stone was regarded, with some justice, as too soft for use in London and although it was employed for the building of St Bartholomew's Hospital, it never gained the reputation that Allen had hoped for. Not that in the end this mattered. In Bath itself there was a demand for stone great enough to make a second fortune for Allen. To meet the local builders' requirements which grew more urgent and massive as Bath's fame developed, he devised an ingenious machine to transport his stone from the heights of Combe Down to the river[12]. This worked by a combination of gravity and pulleys, operated over a trackway following the general line of what is now Ralph Allen Drive. The trucks with their great loads of Allen's stone, rolling slowly down the hillside were to become one of the sights of Bath. When Allen bought his quarries, few new buildings had been completed in Bath. The third of the founding fathers of Bath now makes his appearance.

John Wood, a twenty-year-old surveyor and builder, sent to Allen, perhaps by invitation, a set of plans for the development of Bath. Wood was at the time engaged on work for the Duke of Chandos in London, who was later to employ him in Bath. Little is known of his earlier life, but it seems that he first revealed his talents in the service of Lord Bingley, for whom he did work in

12 Prior Park, with tramway, from a drawing of 1750

Yorkshire. Although little more than a boy, he showed himself to be an expert exponent of the strict classical style now preferred to the exuberance of Wren. It was presumably through Bingley that he was brought to the notice of Chandos, and thus into a world in which Bath played a major rôle. How far Allen encouraged Wood's interest in Bath is not known, but it is reasonable to assume that he would have done so. Certainly Wood received encouragement, for he began at once to enter into preliminary negotiations with Bath landowners, and in 1727, two years after he had sent his proposals to Allen, he moved to Bath, where he was to spend the rest of his life.

Wood was an enthusiast for the newly fashionable style of domestic architecture. The Palladian style, as it was called, was named after Andrea Palladio, a sixteenth-century Italian architect, whose *Quattro Libri dell' Architettura* was based on the *De*

Architectura of Vitruvius, written in 11 BC, and republished in the fifteenth century. Inigo Jones was much influenced by Palladio's interpretation of the classical Roman principles of architecture, but Wren, who succeeded him as the leading English architect, was eclectic in his tastes, and his work, incorporating French, Dutch and Belgian influences as well as that of Palladio, tended towards the Baroque. Wren, however, introduced a method which was to be basic to the work of the builders and architects who followed him, and was used to great effect in Bath. He standardised and simplified construction techniques, enabling local builders to produce without difficulty houses in the true Wren style. In 1715, the Earl of Burlington rebuilt his house in Piccadilly in the Palladian style, and in the same year Colin Campbell began to publish the *Vitruvius Britannicus*, a translation of the Latin work, illustrated with examples of the best classical buildings in Britain. New examples were added over the next ten years, and a host of pattern-books did for the small builder what Wren's earlier publications had done for a previous generation. Wood, as we have seen, was in the van of the new movement. He was moreover a visionary. His plans for Bath envisaged a major transformation of the city; nothing less was in his mind than to turn Bath into the Rome of Britain. We shall see later how his schemes, which included a Forum and a version of the Circus Maximus, fared at the hands of the Corporation. However far his achievement fell short of his dreams, enough was done to establish Wood as the first great architect of Bath and to set a standard by which later builders in the city were guided and are to be measured. If Nash made Bath in the social sense, it was Wood who was its physical creator.

These then are the three men who can properly be claimed as the founders of eighteenth-century Bath. None of them a native of the city (unless, as some have suggested, Wood was born there), they arrived one after the other in the short space of twenty years, at the critical moment for its future development. An ill-assorted trio, each of them made a unique contribution to the history of Bath, a contribution whose value was multiplied by the work of the other two. Nash, the light-weight man of mode, obsessed with good manners and orderly living; Allen, the

13 Ralph Allen's Town House, built in 1727 (*see* p. 39)

sober-minded man of business, combining efficiency and financial drive with a legendary gentleness and modesty of character; Wood, the thrusting and quarrelsome young builder with his obsessive vision of Bath as the new Rome; they can have had little enough in common. It would be wrong to think of them as a triumvirate ruling the city, or even as an unofficial committee of three inspired with a common ambition to make Bath the queen of cities. Apart from the business association of Wood the builder and Allen the quarry-owner, the worlds of the three men barely touched. They came together indeed when they were all involved in some specific undertaking, like the founding of the Mineral Water Hospital, but otherwise each went his own way.

All three were self-made men, in a world in which it was not easy for a man without rank to rise above humble beginnings. In their struggle to achieve eminence and wealth they carried Bath with them to a unique peak of fame and fortune. Of the three only Allen, it appears, was capable of lofty or disinterested aims; and it is not unfair to point out that he had already made one fortune before turning his thoughts to the development of Bath. Neither Nash nor Wood, however, could afford to be altruistic. Perhaps even Allen would have been less enthusiastic about the architectural transformation of Bath if he had not owned the quarries from which the stone for the purpose came. The fact is that if Nash had been less devoted to the interests of his own career as King of Bath; if Wood had been less determined to demonstrate that he was the only Bath architect worthy of the name; or if Allen had been content with his income from the Bye Way and Cross-road posts—if any of this had been so, Bath as we know it would never have happened.

It is also interesting to consider that these three remarkable men devoted their efforts, not to great causes, but to an end commonly held to be trivial and even, for that reason, mildly reprehensible: entertainment and the pursuit of pleasure. The aim of all their work was the provision of facilities for the enjoyment of those who came to Bath with no other purpose. Nevertheless the result of their success, both in the physical and social spheres, was an enduring contribution to human progress and civilisation.

It is all perhaps a good example of the irritating paradox that self-interest, applied with skill and intelligence, is often more productive of good than the disinterested zeal of the reformer. A generation later, Jeremy Bentham was to elevate the paradox into doctrine, and he may well have seen in Bath evidence to support his theories.

III

THE MAKING OF GEORGIAN BATH

Practically nothing remains of the Bath to which Nash came in 1705 with the exception of the Abbey. Only the late medieval houses on the north side of Lilliput Alley now give a faint idea of the appearance of the city at this time. The great houses of the wealthy citizens in Westgate Street have gone. So too have the inns in Stall Street and elsewhere. Of the four city gates only the Eastgate remains, now once more accessible from behind the Guildhall. The medieval wall which followed the general line of the Roman wall is represented only by a small well-preserved section still standing in Upper Borough Walls.

Little building was done in the eighteenth century before John Wood's arrival in 1727, and even less remains. The Saracen's Head in Broad Street has work dating from 1713 and on either side of Green Street there are examples of houses from the same period. There is little else. Even Wood's contemporaries are generally represented only by individual houses. It is John Wood's work that gave Bath its true identity.

Wood's plans for the rebuilding of the city were, as we have indicated, grandiose and indeed visionary; a good deal too visionary for the city fathers, practical, prosperous men of affairs for whom long-term projects had no appeal unless they incorporated a good chance of short-term profit. Wood's vision of

Bath as a latter-day Rome had no such merit. His first proposals included

a grand Place of Assembly to be called the Royal Forum of Bath; another Place, no less magnificent, for the Exhibition of Sports, to be called the Grand Circus; and a third Place, of equal State with either of the former, for the Practice of medicinal Exercises, to be called the Imperial Gymnasium of the City, from a Work of that Kind, taking its rise at first in Bath, during the time of the Roman Emperors.

Later he produced plans for the complete rebuilding of the city. If they were conceived in the same exalted idiom it is perhaps not to be wondered at that the Corporation dismissed his schemes, as he complained, as 'chimerical'.

There is indeed a good deal of absurdity in plans which saw an English spa in terms of a great imperial capital. We may, I think, be content that the city authorities, to Wood's freely expressed scorn, frustrated a scheme which, if it had been realised, might have proved ridiculous. At the same time, in rejecting Wood's proposals, they were giving scope to the architects who followed him and whose individual styles give the city the variety which is one of its great charms.

While his more ambitious plans were being considered, Wood was already busy on more modest undertakings. At the invitation of the Duke of Chandos he completed the rebuilding of St John's Hospital of which the duke held the lease. William Killigrew, a local architect of merit for whom Wood had nothing but contempt, had already rebuilt the chapel—which still stands and may be visited—and had laid the foundations for the remainder of the reconstruction. Working from this basis, which to him was unsatisfactory, Wood succeeded in producing in the hospital and the adjacent Chandos Buildings an architectural achievement of notable quality. Chapel Court, whose north and east sides are Wood's, is one of the most delightful backwaters of Bath. Its dignity and simplicity of design, luckily almost unmarred by later work, provide the earliest example of the powers which were to mark out Wood as the master-architect of the city.

In 1728, the following year, Wood designed a new Assembly House on the Terrace Walk opposite to Harrison's Rooms, with a row of houses to go with it. This Assembly House (known as

Lindsey's and later as Wiltshire's Rooms) has long been demolished and the houses refronted. At the lower end of the Walk, however, the two houses immediately to the north of the entrance to Lilliput Alley, which were built rather later, are much as they originally were, and are fine examples of their period. They flank a narrow passage leading to what remains of Ralph Allen's first house in Bath. Although this house was not designed by Wood, Walter Ison, the authority on the architecture of Georgian Bath, considers that his inspiration is obvious. All that can now be seen is the narrow garden front, a noble façade in a sad state of decay, overdue for the restoration which the city now plans. The house is not open to the public, but the visitor who stands at the entrance to the passage can glimpse it. If he then turns his back on it he can see on the skyline of the opposing hills an extraordinary example of romantic eccentricity on the part of Allen. What at first appears to be a castle is in fact not a building at all, but a mere façade with nothing behind it. Sham Castle, as it is called, was built to Allen's order to add a note of drama to the view from his garden.

While he was engaged on St John's Hospital and Lindsey's Rooms, Wood continued to dream of rebuilding the city on classical lines and to work tenaciously to this end. From the time of his arrival in Bath, he had been negotiating with landowners to acquire ground to the north-west of the city, on which to build in the style and on the scale appropriate to his vision of the new Bath. Within six years he had obtained all the leases he required for what was to be his first great masterpiece. Having drawn up the designs for the exterior of the houses he wished to have built, Wood assumed the rôle of an architectural entrepreneur. Local builders were invited to take individual leases and to build, within Wood's overall design, houses to suit the needs of their prospective clients. Wood's scheme allowed for houses of different sizes and their internal planning was left to the builder concerned, on condition that the exterior remained strictly as Wood had planned it. This was the procedure which he adopted in all his later projects; it involved endless supervision of the builders who tried to save money by omitting or altering decorative details, and arguments with tenants who wanted to introduce their own ideas regardless of the effect on the unity of the whole scheme. Wood was more than a match for them all.

On the land he had leased Wood planned a square, to be named Queen Square, in honour of George II's Queen Caroline. Building began at the beginning of 1729 and went on for seven years. Queen Square is by any standard one of the finest examples of its kind anywhere. Wood's conception was of a palace-front forming the north side of the square, and facing onto a forecourt framed by the east and west sides, which were designed as symmetrical wings. The south side was to complete the picture, playing a subordinate rôle in an unobtrusive style. In the event Wood was not able to realise his plans for the west side, which had to be built as two ranges of houses separated by the forecourt of a large mansion set back from the square. This forecourt is now filled in by a building inserted a century later in a different idiom; although stylistically out of keeping with the rest of the square it is a fine building and closes a gap which was never part of Wood's original conception. The south side of the square was partially destroyed in the 1942 'Baedeker' air-raid on Bath, and the effect of subsequent rebuilding, largely carried out on the original designs, has been marred by unwanted commercial adornments.

The garden in the centre of the square was originally surrounded by a low stone balustrade and divided into symmetrical beds planted with trees and shrubs. Gravel paths led to a central obelisk erected by Nash in honour of the Prince and Princess of Wales in 1738, fellow to the one he had put up in the Orange Grove a few years before. Wood's garden has gone but the obelisk, of which he was extremely proud, still stands in the centre of a pleasant greensward.

Of all the terraces which Wood designed in Bath, there is no doubt that the north side of Queen Square is the finest. With its superb unity of design and grandeur of conception, it dominates the rest of the square. Its south-facing aspect gives it all the light required to show it to advantage. The effect is indeed, as Wood intended, that of a noble palace-front. All Wood's later terraces use a similar formula, the individual houses forming integral components of a single grand design. In this case the

14 Queen Square from the east, as originally built by John Wood the Elder, 1729–36, from a drawing by Thomas Malton the Younger, 1784

15 Queen Square—north side

architect showed his pride in his work by taking the centre house of the north range for himself.

Wood had great plans in mind for the development of the area adjoining Queen Square, eventually to be carried out by his son, but they had to wait for the time being on more pressing tasks to which he now turned. One such task was to design Ralph Allen's great new house at Prior Park, on the outskirts of the city, but this is a story in itself, and is told in Chapter VI.

Another major undertaking was the building of a hospital. The need for an adequate hospital to serve the sick poor who still came to Bath in great numbers had been recognised as early as 1716, when a fruitless effort was made to raise funds for the purpose. In 1723 a second effort met with more success. The announcement of the subscription defined the function of the proposed hospital as the care of 'poor lepers, cripples and other indigent persons resorting to Bath for cure . . . and to discriminate real objects of charity from vagrants and other

16 Obelisk erected by Nash
in the Orange Grove (*see* p. 45)

impostors who crowd both the church and the town to the annoyance of the gentry resorting there'. Nash was one of the four official collectors, and his subscription list, if it was not the longest or fattest, contained more aristocratic names by far than any other; the fact that all the names on his list were ladies is also perhaps not without significance. Enough money was raised at this attempt to make the project seem feasible. Trustees were appointed and a scheme was agreed for a hospital of 150 beds, for which Wood was commissioned to make designs.

The difficulty of finding a site prevented any further progress for over ten years, but the problem was finally solved when public playhouses were suppressed by law in 1737. The existing playhouse was bought for £630 and in the following year building was started. Wood made the hospital a free gift of his plans and his services in directing the building work, which went ahead well enough for the first patients to be admitted four years later. The hospital received the support of a distinguished group of citizens: Dr William Oliver adopted the project as his own and Ralph Allen provided without charge all the stone required for the building, as well as subscribing large sums of money to its funds. The hospital's early history is full of familiar names. Nash was its treasurer from 1738 until his death, collecting in all over £2000 for its support. Dr Oliver, its first president, was succeeded by General Wade, Ralph Allen's patron and father-in-law. Allen himself became president in 1742, to be followed three years later by no less a personage than Frederick, Prince of Wales. The city authorities meanwhile had granted the hospital free use of the Hot Bath and its pumps, and an Act of Parliament to control gambling allocated half the fines collected from offenders to the hospital; facilities and funds were thus available to ensure the future viability of the institution. It is interesting that the original aim of the hospital, to provide for the needs of the indigent sick coming to Bath to seek a cure for their ailments, was adhered to until 1855. Until that date, no citizen of Bath was allowed to be admitted to the hospital. Since its foundation, the hospital has been much extended both in size and function. The Mineral Water Hospital, as it was originally called, is now the Royal National Hospital for Rheumatic Diseases, a clumsy if accurate title. Wood's original design is still largely recognisable; facing north on Upper Borough Walls, its main frontage retains its massive dignity, in spite of the awkward attic storey added in 1793 and the unfortunate omission of glazing-bars in the windows in the recent modernisation.

Soon after the completion of the hospital, Wood was invited to submit plans for a building to house the Free Grammar School. This school, which still flourishes as King Edward's School, was founded in 1553 as one of the schools set up under Edward VI with funds formerly belonging to the church. There is considerable evidence that the city diverted some of the income rightfully belonging to the school to other, doubtless worthy, purposes. It is certainly true that it was ill-housed. In 1583, after the consolidation of the Bath parishes, St Mary's Church by the Northgate became available for secular uses. Its tower was used as a gaol and the nave housed the school. After 150 years of neglect the building was in a scandalously ruinous condition when the Corporation at last decided to provide a new school.

In the event, Wood's plans were not accepted. The city bought the site of the Black Swan in Broad Street and in 1752 the foundation stone of the present building was laid. The designer was Thomas Jelly, to whom the Corporation frequently turned rather than to Wood. It is an excellent Palladian composition, with a lively carving of the city arms in the pediment. The new school was regarded as a municipal foundation separate from the Grammar School which continued to exist, at least in name, in the nave of St Mary's, with its own headmaster. Only on the latter's death were the two schools fused. In 1769 what remained of the church was pulled down to make room for the building of Pulteney Bridge. King Edward's School is now housed in new buildings in North Road, though it still uses the Broad Street building as the Junior School. It is of interest here to record that the only other free public school in Bath at this time was the Blue Coat School, founded as a charity in 1710, and housed in a building in the Sawclose which no longer exists.

The area between the baths and the river had now become established as the social centre of the city. Visitors could drink tea, play cards or dance at one of the two Assembly Houses—

Harrison's and Lindsey's Rooms, to give them their popular names. After taking a glass of the waters in the Pump Room they could amuse themselves on the Bowling Green or take a stroll in Harrison's Walks or the Gravel Walks. The latter area had now been renamed the Orange Grove, in honour of a visit in 1734 by William, Prince of Orange. The prince had been a patient of Dr Oliver and had obtained much benefit from his treatment. In recognition of the honour done to the city by his visit Nash had an obelisk erected in what was now to be called the Orange Grove, with a suitable inscription composed by the doctor. It made an excellent impression.

A much worse impression was made on the visitors by the shortage and inconvenience of lodgings. Wood, as usual, had at least a partial solution. Immediately to the south-east of Harrison's Walks and the Assembly Houses was vacant ground, once the Abbey Orchard, and a marshy area of waste land known as

17 Richard Jones, Ralph Allen, Robert Gay and John Wood by Thomas Hoare, RA (n.d.). Richard Jones was Ralph Allen's Clerk of Works

Ham. Wood had long had plans for the development of this land, and, his work on the hospital now complete, he was able to give them his attention once more. In his own words 'the Circus, intended eight years before for the Ground of the Abbey Orchard, was altered to a Forum to extend southward into the South Part of Ham, as the grand Place of publick Assembly'. The first need, however, was for more lodgings, and in 1739 he began to build an imposing hollow square of terraced houses, fronted to the north by a Grand Parade overlooking the river. Renamed North Parade, as it is still called, it was originally designed much on the lines of the north side of Queen Square, but, under pressure from builders and tenants, a more modest and less striking treatment was in the end imposed. The South Parade on the opposite side of the block fronted onto the proposed site of the Royal Forum. It was therefore provided with its present superbly wide pavement, originally meant as the north promenade of the Forum itself. Its central feature was to be yet another Assembly House, plans for which were discovered only in recent years by Walter Ison, while researching in the city archives of Bristol. Wood's prospectus stated:

The inhabitants of the City of Bath daily increasing, as well as the Resort of Strangers for the Benefit of the Medicinal and Mineral Waters; and the Rooms for publick Assembly being too small for that purpose . . . it is PROPOSED, by John Wood, of the said City, Architect, that a convenient and commodious House shall be erected by Subscription, upon the North side of a Square now begun, and agreed, to be built upon the Abbey Orchard and Ham in the said City . . .

Flanked by dwelling-houses, this Assembly House was to accommodate a large galleried ballroom, a noble drawing-room on the first floor overlooking the Royal Forum, two billiard rooms and a basement theatre. Unhappily neither it nor the Royal Forum itself was ever to be built. Only the great pavement of the South Parade remains as a token of Wood's frustrated schemes.

By 1748 Wood had completed the Parades. His head was still full of plans with which he continuously bombarded both the city authorities and owners of land. He recognised, for example, that the baths themselves, the very source of the city's growing wealth, were totally inadequate and scandalously in need of reconstruction rather than repair. He prepared a comprehensive rebuilding plan but, like almost all the schemes he put to the Corporation, it was rejected out of hand. There seems little room for doubt that the reason why neither Wood nor his son after him was ever given any major civic commission was the jealous opposition of other builders and architects who had the ear of the Corporation; architects like Thomas Atwood, a member of the Common Council and later the City Architect. Undeterred, Wood carried on with private work of brilliant quality.

Gay Street, then known by its old name of Barton Street, leading steeply uphill from the north-east corner of Queen Square, had as yet houses only on its east side, and only as far north as George Street. The lowest house of this range, at the corner of Old King Street, was occupied by John Wood junior. Practically unchanged today and carefully restored, it is a striking building, the corner overlooking Queen Square being constructed as a three-storey bow, pilastered and balustraded and surmounted by a classical urn. It was perhaps in this house that Wood discussed with his son, still in his twenties, the plans for his last and, as many think, his greatest undertaking. The Circus, which had been a central feature of his original plans for the development of the city, had had to give place to the Royal Forum, which in its turn was never built. Wood had nevertheless always nurtured the hope of building it one day, somewhere. Looking towards the empty heights of what was soon to be named Gay Street in honour of its landowner, he saw once more a suitable and even a better site for the great Roman edifice he yearned to build. Plans were made to build houses on the west side of Gay Street and to extend building on both sides of the street as far as a relatively level area beyond the entrance of George Street. This was designed to form a dignified approach to the site, a circular plot over a hundred yards in diameter, of Wood's beloved Circus. With the co-operation of the landowners, and in particular of Robert Gay, the surgeon from whom Wood

18 (*overleaf*) The Circus (built by John Wood the Younger to his father's design), from a drawing by Thomas Malton the Younger, 1784

had earlier leased the ground for Queen Square, plans went ahead fast. He had already agreed to build a house for William Pitt (Nos. 7 and 8 of the present Circus) when in 1754 the first stone was laid. Wood was not to see his dearest dream become reality; within little more than three months he was dead, not yet fifty years old, leaving his son, still under thirty, to put his plans into effect.

Although therefore it was the younger Wood who built the King's Circus, as it was first called, the design was all his father's, and thus it should be described here.

The inspiration for Wood's design was the Roman Colosseum, but he used the basic conception of an amphitheatre in a novel manner and to original effect. Whereas the Roman building is designed to be seen from outside, the Circus faces inward. The exterior of the Colosseum or any of the great Roman amphitheatres is majestic and at times rather grimly impressive. The façades of the Circus are far from grim. The three orders of Roman architecture rise calmly above each other along the curved frontages, richly decorated with masks and garlands, and surmounted by a parapet adorned with stone acorns—a reference to the Bladud legend. The effect is one of superb grace and beauty. The Circus is constructed in three splendid segments, the centre of each facing one of the entrance streets. This feature of the design was a stroke of simple genius. From whatever direction one approaches the Circus, one is faced by an uninterrupted sweep of buildings, with no gap to break the continuity of stone. The central area was originally paved and cobbled, with nothing to obstruct the view of the buildings. The fine trees that now stand there diminish rather than enhance the general effect. Time and the alterations of later builders have taken some of the brilliance from Wood's original creation, but the intrinsic beauty of his design still triumphs, and much faithful restoration has been carried out.

The Circus, unique in conception and superlative in execution, is a fitting culmination to Wood's career as an architect. Twenty years earlier Queen Square had demonstrated his genius. Everything that he produced in the following years confirmed his powers and added to his reputation. Today it is possible to walk from Wood Street through Queen Square, up Gay Street and into the Circus itself and find in this whole area practically no building that is not Wood's. This is John Wood's world, a world of Palladian splendour unsurpassed in England.

Wood so excelled over his contemporaries that it is easy to underestimate them. They made nevertheless their contribution, some of it notable. There was Thomas Greenway who built the group of houses in St John's Court in one of which Nash lived and which earned the rarely bestowed praise of Wood himself. The present entrance to the Theatre Royal disfigures their frontage, but the quality of the building can still be appreciated. Greenway also built, a few yards to the north, Nash's later residence, still known as Beau Nash House. This house, now a restaurant, is exceptionally well-preserved. Its doorway, surmounted by a pair of eagles, is a striking feature, more characteristic perhaps of Nash than Greenway. Other work by Greenway exists in Trim Street and the Abbey Churchyard, if stylistic evidence can be relied upon. General Wolfe's house in Trim Street and General Wade's house in the Abbey Churchyard are early essays by unknown architects in the Palladian style of which Wood was to be the master-exponent.

The work of William Killigrew, a joiner turned architect for whom Wood had nothing but scorn, has largely disappeared, except for the chapel of St John's Hospital already referred to. It had more merit than Wood was ready to admit.

A notable contemporary of Wood's was a Bristol architect named John Strahan. From the spleen with which Wood denigrated his work it may be deduced that he regarded him as an important rival. The decaying remains of Beaufort Square, now in process of restoration, show him to have been an architect of great merit. There is much charm and restraint in their design. Kingsmead Square, which he also planned and built, has been greatly disfigured by later alterations and is almost unrecognisable. One house only, thought to be by Strahan, is of outstanding interest. Rosewell House, on the west side of the square, is quite unlike any other in Bath. Its frontage bears a wealth of baroque decoration in an idiom which must have shocked the exponents of the strict classical style whose work has given Bath its special character. There is however an exuberant gaiety about the figures, masks and scrolls adorning its doorways and windows which is most appealing.

The work of these men which in another town might have given them considerable fame is in Bath quite overshadowed by the achievements of the master. It was he, and he alone, who set Bath on the road, which was to make it in the end, in the words of Ison, 'beyond any question the loveliest of English cities'.

19 Queen Street, through the Trim Street arch

IV

BATH UNDER NASH

While Wood was transforming Bath from a medieval town into
an elegant Georgian city, Nash was engaged on a parallel task in
the social sphere. No longer a mere professional gambler, he had
now taken on his true rôle, that of a legislator of manners and
guardian of public decorum. Not in the least concerned with
standards of morality, he focused his attention on social behaviour. He not only laid down the general principles on which
life at Bath was to be based, but spelt out detailed rules of conduct for those who were ignorant or careless of the conventions
of the day. Goldsmith suspected that he went too far: 'The
solemnity he assumed in adjusting trifles may one day claim the
smile of posterity.' There is justice in this view, but Nash could
have defended his policy at the time with innumerable examples
of minor as well as major offences against good manners.

It is quite clear that the dress and behaviour of the visitors to
Bath at the beginning of the century were frequently rough,
disorderly and coarse. Since entry to Bath society was not
governed by the strict rules applied in London, country squires
or rich merchants, ignorant of the conventions of polite society,
were able to mix freely with visitors from the world of rank and
fashion. For the price of a modest subscription they could attend
the balls and concerts at Harrison's and Lindsey's Rooms and
were free of the Pump Room and the Gardens. Here they rubbed
shoulders with the nobility and had every opportunity of scrap-
ing an acquaintance with them. In the strictly stratified society

of the time, such opportunities were practically non-existent elsewhere and wealthy commoners with marriageable daughters or ambitious wives were only too eager to seize upon them. Ill-bred importunity on the one hand met with offensive rebuffs on the other, and unseemly altercations were all too frequent. Inevitably, standards of manners totally unacceptable in London were tolerated in Bath. Perhaps too the fashionable visitors were glad enough to take a holiday from the restrictive formalities of Town and Court. Even duchesses did not always trouble to wear formal dress in public and were seen in the Pump Room in aprons and without proper headdress. Gentlemen dismounted from their horses and tramped into ballrooms in muddy riding clothes. Gaming, drinking and dancing went on all night or as long as those present could see the cards or stand on their feet. Boisterous horseplay frequently led to quarrels and duelling was commonplace.

In order to control the unruly social scene, Nash took action at two levels, the particular and the general. On detailed matters of dress and conduct he not only expressed to the offender his condemnation in the pungent language of which he was at any time capable, but he published a code of manners which he caused to be posted in all places of public assembly, and which appeared in the annual Bath Guide, from the time of its first publication until years after Nash himself was dead. Nash's rules were a mixture of blunt instructions and didactic memoranda, with a dash of his own brand of insolence to give them point. A few examples will give the flavour:

Gentlemen of Fashion never appearing in a Morning before the Ladies in Gowns and Caps, shew Breeding and Respect.

Gentlemen coming into the Rooms in Boots, where Ladies are, shew their little regard to them or the company
∴ Except they have no shoes.

Ladies dressing and behaving like Handmaids must not be surprised if they are treated as Handmaids.

The last two examples, added by Nash in his old age, suggest that some lessons had to be repeated.

It will already be clear from these short quotations that Nash was no writer. He himself admitted his lack of skill; a pen in his hand, he confessed, was like a torpedo which 'whenever he grasped it, numbed all his faculties'. Nevertheless he was much given to going into print, not only in prose but, more regrettably, in verse. The following lines are among his most successful:

> *Come, trollops and slatterns,*
> *Cockt hats and white aprons,*
> *This best your modesty suits;*
> *For why should not we*
> *In dress be as free*
> *As Hog's Norton squires in boots?*

A torpedo indeed!

There were of course some visitors who objected to being told what to do, when to do it and what to wear when they did it. Others simply found Nash's rules ridiculous. His insolence is referred to by many who were irritated by it, including Alexander Pope who, in a letter of 1714, deplores 'the impudent air of Nash'. Anyone, however, who thought that the officious little Welshman could be ignored or disobeyed with impunity was mistaken. Not only did he mean what he said but offenders, regardless of rank or birth, were publicly and stingingly rebuked.

Princess Amelia, George II's hoydenish and eccentric daughter, who gambled, swore and rode like a man, was firmly refused an extra dance by Nash after the clock had struck eleven, and was not pleased. But she so far forgave him as to present him a silver tureen when she left Bath. Moreover she continued to come to Bath, making seven visits in all. On her later visits she 'sat almost daily in a summer house with two fireplaces by the river, dressed in riding habit and black velvet postillion hat', perhaps a small gesture of defiance, though Nash was dead by then. The Duchess of Queensberry, who appeared at the Rooms in an apron, was sharply rebuked and told that 'such things are suitable for Abigails'. She meekly begged 'His Majesty's' pardon, and did not even plead, as she might have done, that the apron was of the finest lace and worth £200.

Only the eccentric Lord Peterborough successfully ignored the rules; not even Nash could prevent him from wearing riding boots on all occasions. A strange figure who did his own marketing and was to be seen in the street wearing the blue riband and star of the Garter, with a cabbage under each arm and a chicken swinging from his hand, he was the necessary exception proving the rule.

Nash's energies were only partly absorbed by details of social deportment. He saw the need for more general reforms and took steps to introduce and enforce them. The mania for gambling was a serious national problem, to solve which Parliament passed a number of only partially effective measures. It would have been calamitous for Nash if gaming had been stamped out, since it was his main source of income all his life. (When towards the end of his life this happened, he was a broken man.) It was, however, important both to him personally and to Bath as a resort for the well-born and well-bred that gambling in the city should be conducted in an orderly and moderate manner. Without entirely succeeding, he did what he could, by banning private parties and attempting to control high play, to ensure that gaming in Bath had at least a respectable image, whatever the truth of the matter was.

Perhaps Nash's concern for the niceties of behaviour and his insistence on orderly conduct is not particularly remarkable in a Master of Ceremonies whose duty it was by virtue of his office to occupy himself with these matters; only the energy he applied to the task, and the unique methods he employed are worthy of note. Two aspects of his work as King of Bath, however, show him to have possessed an almost prophetic awareness of the direction in which society, though still unwillingly, was moving.

First, he banned duelling, and went so far as to forbid the wearing of swords in the city. At this period swords were normal items of outdoor dress; to carry a sword was the mark of a gentleman, as indispensable to him as the less lethal umbrella is to the Guards officer in London today. Nor was a sword merely an adornment. It was drawn as a protection against footpads and it lent zest to the brawls which not infrequently followed gaming or drinking parties. It was also used for duelling. Nash was right to think that the way to stamp out duelling was to forbid the wearing of the duelling weapon. His objection to duels was on a footing with his distaste for any behaviour which was uncouth or impolite, and what could be more so than a sword-wound rudely inflicted and certain to bleed in an unseemly manner? Before imposing his ban, Nash had to forestall the imputation of cowardice, and he therefore held his hand until he himself had contrived a suitable occasion to fight a duel. When at the Cross Bath a gentleman in full dress rhapsodised immoderately over the physical charms of his wife which were on generous display in the water, Nash seized the opportunity of pushing him into the bath with her. The ensuing duel was a half-hearted affair, much exaggerated by Nash afterwards, but it was good enough. He imposed his ban. 'None should ever wear a sword in Bath but such who were not entitled to wear it elsewhere', as he expressed it, with more point than grace. The ill-phrased enactment was clear enough and Nash was obeyed as usual. Resentfully in some cases, but generally with a wry good humour, gentlemen went unarmed. So rigid and lastingly effective was the ban that more than 50 years later Captain Absolute in Sheridan's *The Rivals*, setting out for his famous duel, was still constrained to hide his sword under his greatcoat. In spite of Nash duels were, of course, still arranged and some were fought, but the city authorities co-operated with the Master of Ceremonies and acted vigorously whenever news of an impending meeting leaked out. Many were thus prevented.

It is on this account that Nash takes his place in history. For the rule that he introduced and enforced in Bath was copied in other watering-places in England and on the Continent and at last became the practice in London. The sword ceased to be generally worn and duelling slowly fell into disuse. In the following century it was widespread only in military circles. There is no doubt that the disappearance of this stupid practice was greatly accelerated by the initiative of Nash.

His second contribution to social progress has only in the present century become an accepted part of civilised life. He saw, and was one of the very few to see, that snobbery based on birth was unacceptable in a situation in which different social classes had to come into close contact with each other, as was inevitable at Bath in the Pump Room or at the twice-weekly balls. For Nash, though he insisted that the respect due to rank should be shown, all private visitors to Bath were in a sense his guests and entitled to be treated with courtesy. He would not tolerate rudeness on the part of the aristocracy to fellow guests of lower station. A peeress who, at a ball, gave only the tips of her fingers to a partner of common birth, instead of the whole hand which convention required, would be asked firmly, and not always very politely, to leave. Nash's rules for good behaviour no doubt assisted the less socially cultivated visitor to avoid the worst errors, but they were not in themselves the whole answer. What was needed was plenty of practice in the novel art of mixing with one's social unequals. With the calm effrontery which made him so formidable, Nash simply banned all forms of private entertainment. Life in Bath, he made clear, was to be lived in public. The countess who wished to keep to her own select circle of friends and avoid contact with the mere gentry at the Assembly Rooms, and the country squire who preferred a rowdy drinking party in his lodgings to the politenesses of the ballroom came equally under the proscription of the all-powerful Master of Ceremonies. With good or ill grace, the visitors had to bow before his ruling.

Before Nash's day Goldsmith tells us, 'the nobility still preserved a tincture of Gothic haughtiness, and refused to keep company with the gentry at any of the public entertainments of the place'. As early as 1712, however, Nash's success in fusing the different elements of Bath society into a harmonious whole received favourable comment from Steele, the essayist and social commentator. Dr Oliver, who wrote the customary eulogy on Nash's death, praised him for discovering the 'happy secret of uniting the vulgar and the great'. Goldsmith's assessment of his achievement, written the year after Nash's death, was based on his personal experience of Bath and London society. 'He first taught', he writes, 'a familiar intercourse among strangers at Bath and Tunbridge, which still subsists among them. That ease and open access first acquired there, our gentry brought back to the metropolis, and thus the whole kingdom by degrees became more refined by lessons originally derived from him.'

Just as Nash's kingdom was ruled by the laws he had

established, so a visit to Bath was governed by customs having almost the force of law. A fixed procedure operated from arrival to departure. Events and activities followed each other in a pre-scribed order like the steps in a minuet. Protocol came into force before the visitor had in fact arrived. By an effective intelligence system the appearance of any coach at the outskirts of the city was notified, with the names of the occupants, to the spa authorities. Regardless of the hour of day or night, a peal of bells was then played to welcome them. The complaints of the in-valids whose rest was disturbed by this practice were loud, frequent and completely ignored. They were now in the minority, and the identity and rank of all new arrivals were matters of overriding concern to the holiday-makers who outnumbered them. The lodging-house keepers and tradesmen, not to mention the professional gamesters, were also vitally interested in getting early information of the social and financial status of new cus-tomers, provisionally assessed by the style of the equipage which brought them and the number of their servants. The ringing of bells enabled this information to be readily obtained. In spite of criticism this practice continued long after Nash had died. Philip Thicknesse, writing in 1778, has a sharp comment:

The etiquette is that, whoever enters Bath with a Set of Horses, their Arrival must be announced by the clappers of Four-and-twenty Bells, while Two Hundred miserable Sick are to be tortured by them.

Having found his lodgings, the visitor, generally exhausted by a long journey over appalling roads, was then assailed by the city waits, who provided a serenade at a fee of half a guinea for a nobleman or five shillings for a commoner. The bell-ringers would now also demand payment—a guinea if the visitor had a title, half a guinea otherwise. Other dues had to be paid, and the earlier the better. The most important was the subscription to the Assembly Rooms, two guineas including admission to the balls, one guinea excluding this but with the use of the public gardens. It was also usual to join one of the subscription libraries, where the London newspapers could be read, books could be borrowed and letters written: the charge was a guinea for a

20 Patients in trouble, with Royal Crescent in the background,
by Thomas Rowlandson from 'The Comforts of Bath', 1798

nobleman and five shillings for a commoner, with an extra fee for the use of pens and writing-paper.

At an early stage a formal call on the Master of Ceremonies was incumbent on the visitor who wished his presence to be socially recognised, and Nash made a return call on those he thought it appropriate to welcome personally. If, at the height of the season, this was not in every case possible, he took the first opportunity of making their acquaintance on a public occasion. This was an essential indication of social acceptability. Thereafter the visitors could be sure of a bow from the great man when they appeared in the Rooms or were seen by him in the street, and would be introduced to the right people as occasion offered. If it did not happen, the implication was that Nash did not wish to know the newcomers, and they had thus little chance of finding a place in Bath society. The publicity given to all new arrivals made it only too clear to those who did not receive a welcome from the Beau that the omission was deliberate: a brutal indication of social undesirability.

It was not mandatory upon the visitor to frequent the baths and more stayed away than went. Those who did go went in the early morning. In seemly but informal dress, usually a dressing-gown, the bather was taken by sedan chair to the King's, Queen's or Cross Bath, the Queen's Bath being for ladies only, and thus used only by those for whom bathing had a therapeutic rather than a social purpose. The Cross Bath was the one most frequented by the quality, for enjoyment rather than for medical reasons. In the 'slips' or dressing rooms, the visitor was helped into bathing clothes by an attendant: canvas drawers and waist-coats for the men and a capacious dress for the women with sleeves like a parson's gown which, as the modest Celia Fiennes had gratefully recorded a few years earlier, 'was quickly filled up with water, thus disguising the shape'. Guides, their skins tanned by constant immersion in the hot mineral waters, steered the bathers and held them upright until they found their balance. Ladies received from an attendant 'a little floating dish like a bason, into which the lady puts an handkerchief, a snuff-box and a nosegay'. Once on a firm footing the bathers amused themselves as they felt inclined. As men and women, to the disgust of the prudish, bathed together, there was plenty of interest to occupy everybody, and if at times the limits of propriety were exceeded, little exception was taken. A pamphlet called 'A Step to the Bath with a Charade of the Place', written a little before Nash's day, gives a vivid picture of the Cross Bath which was no doubt still in the main valid:

Here is perform'd all the Wanton Dalliance imaginable; Celebrated Beauties, Panting Breasts, and Curious Shapes, almost expos'd to Public View; Languishing Eyes, Darting Glances, Tempting Amorous Postures, attended by soft Musick, enough to provoke a Vestal to forbidden Pleasures. . . . Here were also different Sexes, from Quality to the Honourable Knights, Country Puts and City Madams.

After an hour or so in the bath it was time to leave. In the slips the cloth-women were waiting to dry and dress the bather. This process is acidly described by Thicknesse:

Neither sex can come out of the King's Bath without being stripped quite naked by an old woman, who takes off the wet, and put on dry Apparel: for our part, we think, being thus stripped by an old Hagg, alive, is but little better than being served the same Sauce when dead in the Field of Battle.

After submitting to this undignified treatment and paying the proper dues (3*d*. to the Serjeant of the Baths, 1*s*. to the Guide and 3*d*. to the Cloth-woman) the bathers, wrapped in blankets, were taken back to their lodgings. Here they went sweating to bed and, when sufficiently cooled, got dressed and went out to breakfast. This could be taken either in a coffee-house or, by crossing the river by ferry, in a pavilion in Spring Gardens. Here there was music, and it was fashionable to hold large breakfast parties in this romantic outdoor setting.

From eight to nine o'clock was the time for the ritual visit to the Pump Room to drink the waters (three glasses were prescribed) and meet one's friends. The custom survives to the present day, though one glass of medicinal water is generally found sufficient. The flavour of the water has been variously described: one enthusiast compared it with Beaune, but Dickens' Sam Weller thought it had 'a wery strong flavour o' warm flat irons'. At any rate it was drunk, whether with pleasure or disgust,

21 Pump Room scene by Thomas Rowlandson
from 'The Comforts of Bath', 1798

and the Pump Room provided a convenient social focus for the early part of the day. The ladies now dispersed to their lodgings or to the coffee-houses, while the gentlemen strolled towards the libraries and reading-rooms to glance at the journals and discuss the news. Some of these libraries survived well into the following century as bookshops and there is the original advertisement of one of them, in the form of fading lettering, to be seen on the wall of No. 43 Milsom Street, on the east side of the road. Until 1744 Bath had no newspaper of its own; then the *Bath Journal* appeared, a short-lived weekly. In 1760 a new journal called by various names, but from 1770 entitled the *Bath Chronicle*, took over and was joined in 1792 by the *Bath Herald*. The *Chronicle* was also a weekly, costing 2½d. and consisting of four closely printed pages without headlines. It published home and foreign news received from London, and Parliamentary reports. Only half a column was devoted to events in Bath. Here there were announcements of entertainments and, most important, a list of arrivals. The *Chronicle* and the *Herald*, together with a revived *Journal*, continued to appear until the present century. The *Journal* was then absorbed by the *Herald*, which was itself amalgamated in 1925 with the *Chronicle*. The latter continues to appear as a thriving daily, under the title of *The Bath and Wilts Evening Chronicle*. Until the Second World War it continued to publish lists of arrivals at the spa.

At midday it was the custom to go to church, at the Abbey for preference. Here the congregation consisted mainly of visitors, whereas the numerous parish churches, although more conveniently sited for their lodgings, served largely the citizens of Bath, and were thus socially less interesting. To meet the wish of visitors to worship God in the company of their peers, as well as to cater for the increased population of the newly-built areas of the city, John Wood had offered to rebuild, partly at his own expense, the church of St Michael-extra-Muros, on condition that a section of pews were reserved for residents of Queen Square. The parishioners rejected this condition. Wood therefore built a private chapel, St Mary's, at the south-west corner of the square, for the exclusive use of residents, who were alone allowed to rent a pew, at a figure which effectively excluded the ordinary citizen.

This chapel, opened in 1734, was the first of the proprietary chapels in Bath. Five more were to be built, and they, and the system, strange to modern thinking, under which they were established, are described in Chapter VII.

After dinner, usually taken at three o'clock, a general lull set in until the evening entertainments began. These consisted of card-playing, dancing, playgoing or concerts. Both Assembly Houses had card-rooms, which were always full. The same cannot be said of the theatre. The playhouse, an entirely inadequate building, was in Borough Walls. Built by subscription in the early years of the century it bore, on a frieze round the walls of the auditorium, the coats of arms of those who had contributed. The performances were, however, less distinguished than the lineage of the subscribers and were poorly patronised. Chester-field records an audience of seventeen in 1734. Two years later an Act of Parliament suppressed public playhouses and the Bath theatre closed its doors; on its site the Mineral Water Hospital was shortly to be built. Thereafter plays were performed in the cellar of Simpson's Rooms and occasionally in the yard of one of the city's inns. In 1750, after the Act was repealed, a new theatre was built in Orchard Street, based on plans by John Wood, but designed probably by Thomas Jelly, one of Wood's most active competitors. In this theatre, Sarah Siddons was to make her name, and the theatre itself was later granted the title of Theatre Royal, the first theatre outside London to be granted this honour. For the time being however the stage competed ill with the other attractions of Bath.

Nash's modest band of six musicians was soon expanded into a city orchestra and subscription concerts became an important and permanent feature of the entertainment provided for the visitor.

For those with a taste neither for music nor the theatre, and these were in the majority, the two Assembly Houses provided more frivolous activities. The Rooms each opened on alternate days, Simpson's on Tuesdays, Thursdays and Saturdays and Wiltshire's on Mondays, Wednesdays and Fridays. The weekly ball at Simpson's was on Tuesday and at Wiltshire's on Friday. There was thus no evening when it was impossible to find entertainment. Above all, the national pastime of gambling could be pursued without pause. It was all very convenient, if somewhat repetitive. The twice-weekly balls were the main events of the social programme. They were highly formal occasions, starting promptly at six and ending, as we have seen, on the stroke of eleven. The lady of highest rank present was first led out by the Master of Ceremonies to dance a minuet. In strict order of precedence other couples then took the floor, each pair dancing alone. For the débutante of the day the ordeal of performing such a duet under the critical eye of a large assembly was admitted to be one of the major pains of 'coming out'. After an interval for refreshment (tea was the fashionable drink) a programme of country dances followed, in which all joined. These were not country dances in the modern sense, but 'contredanses', so-called because the dancers formed up in line facing each other.

Of the two Assembly Houses, Harrison's or Simpson's was the original and larger. Built under Nash's pressure in 1708, it contained two tea-rooms, a good-sized card-room and a spacious ballroom. Its position overlooking Harrison's Walks with a view of the river and the hills beyond was one of its most attractive features. Lindsey's Rooms, designed by John Wood in 1728, stood on the opposite side of the Terrace Walk, in a less favourable position than its competitor, and was smaller. Both Houses changed hands more than once in Nash's time and later, and each new tenant gave the Rooms his name, to the frequent bewilderment of the modern student. The first tenant of the Rooms designed by Wood was Dame Lindsey, a retired singer of some notoriety. Lindsey's Rooms were taken over on her death in 1737 by Wiltshire, with whom Nash was to go to law on a notable occasion which will be described later. Wiltshire's Rooms declined irrevocably when the Upper Rooms (the present Assembly Rooms) were opened in 1771, and they were used as a warehouse until they were demolished to make way for the construction of York Street in the early nineteenth century.

On Harrison's death in 1735 his Rooms were taken over by Dame Lindsey's sister, who became Lady Hawes, and later by Simpson. In 1749 Simpson enlarged and improved his establishment, which was usually known as the Lower Rooms, by adding a theatre in the basement. Unlike Wiltshire's Rooms, Simpson's continued to thrive until they were destroyed by fire in 1820. Significantly, portraits of Nash hung in Wiltshire's Rooms and in both the ballroom and card-room at Simpson's. They symbolised, perhaps by design, the sharp watch he kept on everything that went on in each establishment.

There is no doubt that for those who were content to pass their time in a prescribed round of activities, moving from one scene to another as if at the ringing of a bell by the Master of Ceremonies, Bath with its new Pump Room, its Assembly Houses, its concerts and its promenades, its growing number of elegant lodgings, was an extremely pleasant place. Not only was everything done on the whole in a civilised manner, but it was done in public where it could be seen to be civilised. To us, for whom privacy is precious and increasingly hard to come by, Nash's insistence on a communal social life seems strange. But at a time when travel was slow and dangerous and all forms of communication difficult, opportunities to enjoy the company of others were correspondingly rare. Without trains and motor cars, or the contact provided by the telephone, television and an efficient press, the eighteenth century lived in a degree of isolation hard for us to imagine. Perhaps the greatest amenity which Bath offered, and which Nash instinctively understood and fostered, was the opportunity to meet one's fellow human beings freely, easily and in comfort, under conditions of decency and dignity. For this purpose the regularity of the daily routine was of central importance: at any time of day one knew where to find one's friends, or how, if need be, to avoid them. Lydia Melford, the heroine of Smollett's *Humphrey Clinker*, describes in a letter to a friend how her day was passed at Bath:

At eight in the morning we go in dishabille to the Pump-room which is crowded like a Welsh fair; and there you see the highest quality, and the lowest trades folks, jostling each other, without ceremony, hail-fellow well-met. . . . Right under the Pump-room windows is the King's Bath: a huge cistern, where you see the patients up to their necks in hot water. The ladies wear jackets and petticoats of brown linen, with chip hats, in which they fix their handkerchiefs to wipe the sweat from their faces. . . . My aunt, who says every person of fashion should make her appearance in the bath, as well as in the abbey church, has contrived a cap with cherry-coloured ribbons to suit her complexion. . . . For my part, I content myself with drinking about half a pint of water every morning. . . .

Hard by the Pump-room, is a coffee-house for the ladies, but my aunt says, young girls are not admitted, inasmuch as the conversation turns upon politics, scandal, philosophy, and other subjects above our capacity; but we are allowed to accompany them to the booksellers' shops, which are charming places of resort; where we read novels, plays, pamphlets, and news-papers, for so small a subscription as a crown a quarter; and in these offices of intelligence (as my brother calls them), all the reports of the day, and all the private transactions of the Bath, are first entered and discussed. From the bookseller's shop, we make a tour through the milliners and toy-men; and commonly stop at Mr Gill's, the pastry-cook, to take a jelly, a tart, or a small bason of vermicelli. There is, moreover, another place of entertainment on the other side of the water, opposite to the Grove; to which the company cross over in a boat. It is called Spring Garden; a sweet retreat, laid out in walks and ponds, and parterres of flowers; and there is a long-room for breakfasting and dancing. . . . I have been twice at the play. . . .

The great scenes of entertainment at Bath are the two public rooms; where the company meet alternately every evening. They are spacious, lofty, and, when lighted up, appear very striking. They are generally crowded with well-dressed people, who drink tea in separate parties, play at cards, walk or sit and chat together, just as they are disposed. Twice a week there is a ball; the expense of which is defrayed by a voluntary subscription among the gentlemen; and every subscriber has three tickets. I was there Friday last with my aunt. . . . The place was so hot . . . that I was quite feverish when we came away.

Miss Melford, a well-bred and docile young woman, conformed happily with the conventions of life at Bath; not everyone was so amenable. Nash's social system required his personal supervision and rigid control to maintain it. Without this, it could easily break down, as indeed it began to do immediately after his death. There was so much that was new and unfamiliar in the Bath social code that it required the exercise of an absolute and ruthless authority to make it work. Nash supplied this. He was in fact as well as in name the King of Bath. Within the narrow territory over which he ruled, his power was greater, more arbitrary and more freely recognised than that exercised over the nation as a whole by the Hanoverian who occupied the throne. He was his own Walpole. He founded no dynasty, it is true, but for 100 years the after-effects of his policies can be traced in the history of England.

Without misusing language, it can be said that eighteenth-century Bath was a work of art, and that Richard Nash was the artist. The Bath which we see today, with its elegant crescents and parades, forms the setting appropriate to the life he created. It is the décor for his operetta.

Bath pavement

V

RICHARD NASH

To understand the Bath that Nash created it is essential to understand something of Nash himself. 'All admired him as an extraordinary character', said Goldsmith in the *Life*, 'and some, who knew no better, as a fine gentleman.' The statement stimulates curiosity without satisfying it. How was it that a man in his early thirties, with neither rank nor wealth, was able first to establish and then to maintain, for most of a long life, a position of unchallenged dominance in a world to which he had in fact not even the right of entry?

To be a square peg in a round hole carries no suggestion that the hole is the wrong shape. Roundness is the proper characteristic of a hole. It is the peg which is at fault; its corners must be rubbed off until it fits. That, at least, is the natural implication of the metaphor. Nash was a very queer-shaped peg indeed, and no available hole existed into which he could comfortably fit himself. Temperamentally incapable of adjusting himself, he set to work to adjust his surroundings. It is a commonplace to assert that artists are generally misfits, and if this is true Nash had at least one of the qualities of an artist. Uncomfortable in the world in which he found himself, he set about creating a world more to his liking, a small one perhaps, but one into which he managed to build the features necessary for his contentment. This world was as truly a work of art as a ballet or a group of statuary. And like any other important work of art its impact was powerful and its effect irreversible. What sort of man was its author?

Nash was born in 1674, the son of a Swansea bottle-maker, a man of humble birth carrying on without distinction an undistinguished trade. When, in a passing period of prosperity, he sent his son to Oxford, to Jesus College, the proper place for a Welshman, he was accurately designated 'pleb' in the college records. Goldsmith says that 'his father was a gentleman', but this is the amiable exaggeration of a biographer. The year Nash spent at Oxford gave him his first contact with a fashionable world to which he did not belong by birth, but which was then, as it generally has been, open to men of talent and charm. Nash's first sight of this new world did not, as it might have done, fill him with awe. He greeted it instead with recognition; he felt this was where he truly belonged, and he set about establishing his claims to membership. He adopted easily the usual ways of his better-born fellow undergraduates, and was sent down in the usual way for the usual reason: a scandalous affair with a woman. He left behind the traditional debts and, for some unexplained reason, his fiddle. He had meanwhile acquired sufficient social graces and friends of the right kind to enable him to obtain a commission in the Guards. (In later years, Boswell, with more initial advantages by way of birth and wealth, never succeeded in spite of strenuous and protracted efforts, in achieving this high ambition.) The Army offered a man like Nash a great deal which he lacked: a rank which placed him unmistakably in a social category acceptable in the highest circles, a scarlet uniform to cover up the drabness of his origins and in which he could confidently act the role of gallant, and the glamour which has always attracted women to the military. But it was a very expensive life and this is perhaps why, after only a year, he resigned.

To obtain a lot of money quickly and at the same time to have plenty of leisure in which to enjoy it was central to Nash's plan of life, and was to be a chronic preoccupation all his days. It was therefore a false step for him to join the Inner Temple, as he now did. It is impossible to imagine him as a lawyer; nor is there any evidence that he attempted seriously to qualify as one. Instead he devoted himself assiduously to his true calling: gambling. It was as a law student that he learned to play cards well enough to win fairly consistently. He had to win, not only in order to play again, but so as to cut a figure in a society which, though less magnificent than the Guards, had expensive ways. 'He was now,' writes Goldsmith, 'by profession a gamester.' If he was also technically a law student, it was not the statutes of the land that he studied, but the laws of chance; laws that, unlike the man-made regulations which were the business of the courts, required no officers to enforce compliance, no magistrates to assess the penalty for their breach, and left no loopholes for learned argument. The laws which Nash studied with such success and on which he became an authority, incorporated their own penalties, were infallibly just, and allowed no mercy to the offender. But just as the offender is punished, so the student who masters their intricacies is well paid for his efforts. Nash lived, and lived well, by his knowledge of, and respect for, the laws of chance. 'He went,' says Goldsmith in his *Life of Nash*, 'to the very summit of second-rate luxury.' In later life he was to give constant warning to those who thought they could bend these laws to their own advantage, and tried, usually in vain, to prevent foolish young gentlemen from attempting this impossible task. At the Inner Temple Nash earned himself the ironical title of 'The Count', a not very unlikely honorific for a man who all his life was a flamboyant and arrogant figure. 'Though very poor he was very fine,' says Goldsmith of him at this time.

Throughout Nash's life, whatever he did seemed to attract attention and this characteristic was already noticeable. Any young man is liable to fall hopelessly in love, as Nash did with a Miss Verdun; some would be quixotic enough, as he was, to persuade the lady's father, when he knew his own cause was lost, to allow her to marry the man of her choice. But few would find their misadventure the subject of a play by a leading dramatist. Nash's love affair, however, was made the basis of Vanbrugh's play *Aesop* and Cibber took the leading rôle when it was performed. Elected Treasurer of his Inn, Nash showed the generosity which was one of his amiable features in a typically eccentric manner. Meeting a needy fellow in the Temple, who told him that £10 would make him happy for life, Nash supplied him with this sum on the spot. It is in keeping with his character that he later charged this sum to his Inn, marking the entry 'To making a man happy for life—ten pounds'. To their credit, the Inn agreed the item, and even, according to Goldsmith, doubled it.

It was while still a law student that Nash supplied the first recorded evidence of his extraordinary gift for social organisation. In 1695 Queen Mary, wife of William III, died, and a fresh coronation was held to mark the King's accession to the throne in his own right. Nash was given the task of arranging an entertainment to be offered to the King by the Inner Temple in honour of this event. So successful was the affair and the monarch so delighted that, in an expansive moment, he offered Nash an immediate knighthood. Nash had the sense to refuse.

In spite of apparent triumphs of this kind, we are still entitled to think of Nash as a misfit. The law was no more his *métier* than the Army had been and the Inns of Court not affluent enough to bring him an adequate return for his skill as a gambler. He needed a more profitable sphere and one was in fact available. When Queen Anne's gout drove her to Bath, not once but twice, in search of relief she was, of course, accompanied by her court and its hangers-on. Whatever the effect of the waters on the Queen's feet, the effect of the royal patronage on Bath was immediate and dramatic. It became in no time the fashionable resort *par excellence*. A steady migration of professional gamblers to Bath began and in 1705 Nash joined it. It was a logical step. If a fortune were to be made at the tables, it would be at those frequented by the nobility in holiday mood. We have already seen that he made an immediate hit and was within an astonishingly short time in a position of unique authority in the town, to which he had come with no hope beyond the prospect of winning a regular income commensurate with his requirements. His public career as Master of Ceremonies is so much the same thing as the rise of Bath itself as a resort of fashion that it can be better dealt with in that context. Here we are concerned with his personal life and the impression he made on those who knew him. For this, there is a mass of evidence, some of it reliable, a huge store of anecdotes, most of them scandalous but others oddly moving, and a considerable mythology, largely originating with Nash himself. Here we shall try to find our way through it all.

The anonymous author of the *Characters at the Hot Well, Bristol, in September and at Bath, in October 1723* gives the first authentic description of the way he looked at the height of his career, referring to his 'very agreeable oddness of appearance—black wig, white hat, scarlet countenance and brown beaver habit'. He amplifies the picture, with more than a dash of flattery, as follows:

Mr Nash is a man about five feet eight inches high, of a diameter exactly proportioned to your [sic] height, that gives you the finest shape; of a black-brown complexion that gives a strength to your looks suited to the elastic force of your nervous fibres and muscles. You have enough strength and agility to recommend you to your own sex, and great comeliness of person to keep you from being disagreeable to the other. You have heightened a great degree of natural good temper by cultivating the greatest politeness which, improved with natural good wit, makes your conversation as a private person as entertaining and as delightful as your authority as a governor is respectful.

The white hat and red face were to be Nash's most notable features until the end. In 1743, his seventieth year, he was described (no flattery here) as a 'silly overlord, a wornout and toothless old man, crowned with a white hat and whose face was animated iron rust, changeless and shameless red'.

In his dress he showed a Jacobean taste for the flamboyant which was out of keeping with the sober preferences of the Georgian gentleman. In 1734, Chesterfield was present at a ball he gave at the Assembly Rooms when Nash wore his gold-laced clothes and 'was taken by many at a distance for a gilt garland'. He habitually wore a diamond buckle in his stock and a diamond star to pin back the brim of his hat, a Stuart style no longer approved. It is strange that a man of fashion, such as Nash essentially was, should not keep up with it; one can only suppose that his love of personal display was stronger than his desire to be in the mode, particularly when the mode was simplicity and sobriety. 'Wit, flattery and fine cloaths,' Goldsmith quotes him as saying, 'are enough to debauch a nunnery.' His love of splendour also expressed itself in his equipage, much in evidence on his regular trips to Tunbridge Wells, where he was also a part-time Master of Ceremonies. He was, at the height of his insecure

22 Prince Hoare's statue of Nash, in the Pump Room

affluence, the owner of a coach and six greys 'so well matched and paced so well together when in full trot that any person at a distance would imagine it was only one horse that drew the carriage'. He took with him on his travels a coachman and postillion, two footmen, outriders with French horns, a gentleman out of livery and Bryan, his famous Irish running footman. Few noblemen could have done better than that; not many, perhaps, would have wished to. It was really on the whole a bit excessive for anyone less than a duke.

In keeping with the style of his dress and carriage was his house, the fine mansion in St John's Court, newly built in 1720 as one of a group of four by Greenway. Here in 1740 he entertained Princess Mary, a daughter of George II, when a fire at Hetling House prevented her lodging there. Here, too, he kept his mistress Fanny Murray, the daughter of a local musician. Miss Murray remained with him in this capacity for many years until he replaced her by Juliana Papjoy, a dressmaker who also followed, in her spare time, the innocent pursuit of simpling or herb-gathering. He presented his new mistress with a dapple-grey horse and a remarkable whip with multiple thongs, hence her popular name of 'Lady Betty Besom'. It should not be thought because of his irregular domestic arrangements that Nash was, by contemporary standards, a man of immoral life. His verdict on himself in this context can be accepted. 'A man can no more be termed a whoremonger for having one whore in his house than a cheesemonger for having one cheese.'

This remark is one of the better examples of Nash's wit. His reputation in this field rests on shaky foundations. What passed for epigrams were often nothing more than impudences, and at times show a good deal of cruelty. When a crippled lady informed him that she had come 'straight from London', he is said to have replied 'Confound me, Madam, then you must have been damnably warped on the way.' This story figures in Smollett's *Roderick Random*, in the context of the hero's pursuit of the rich but deformed Miss Snapper. Goldsmith affirms, however, that it was a true story. 'Nash,' says Goldsmith, 'was really agreeable, but chose to be thought a wit,' and adds, 'Of all the jests recorded of him, I scarce find one that is not marked with petulance.' In an effort to be scrupulously fair, he admits elsewhere that 'once a week he might say a good thing'. Perhaps one epigram a week is as much as can be expected from anyone; at all events, Nash regarded himself as a wit, and the opinion was generally shared.

At the height of his fame, Nash was treated with all the adulation which he plainly considered his due. The nobility flattered and deferred to him. He was showered with compliments and gifts, especially snuff-boxes. Both Frederick, Prince of Wales, and William, Prince of Orange, had given him gold enamelled snuff-boxes as parting gifts, and it became the practice for others to do so. He amassed a large collection, which he was able to dispose of piecemeal at times of financial stress in his later years. His portraits appeared everywhere. One, either presented by Nash himself or commissioned by the Corporation, showing the subject at full length, was hung in the Rooms. It was flanked originally by busts of Newton and Pope. The absurdity of the juxtaposition was irresistible to the wits, and particularly to Chesterfield. The lines attributed to him on the subject could not be more apt:

> *Immortal Newton never spoke*
> *More truth than here you'll find,*
> *Nor Pope himself e'er penned a joke*
> *Severer on mankind.*
>
> *The picture placed, the busts between,*
> *Adds to the satire strength;*
> Wisdom *and* Wit *are little seen,*
> *But* Folly *at full length.*

As Master of Ceremonies, Nash received no salary; the theory was that the perquisites attached to the appointment, particularly through the patronage of which the incumbent disposed, were payment enough. They were not, of course, enough for Nash, who still had to depend on gambling to supply his large requirements. We do not know how big his income was from this source, and of course he did not always win. The Countess of Bristol, a mistress of George II, who was an habituée of Bath at this time, and a busy letter-writer, wrote to a friend on one occasion 'Mr Nash lost £50 a Saturday at Harrison's and as they say broke all the windows according to custom.' But in the main he must have won and won heavily. As far as we know he also won fairly. Although the card-sharpers of Bath are notorious in the literature of the time, it is never hinted that Nash was one of them. He won, we must believe, by his superior skill. At the same time he was at pains to conceal the size and consistency of his winnings, not only to preserve the fiction that he, like any other gentleman, played simply for amusement, but also in order not to scare away those destined to provide his future income. Nash's pose as a man of independent means did not, however, deceive everyone. When on one occasion he lamented to Lord Chesterfield that he had lost £500 at a sitting and professed his astonishment at his own bad luck, Chesterfield, who was nobody's fool, retorted that he did not wonder at his losing money, but that 'all the world is surprised where you get it to lose'.

Everyone gambled; it was the main amusement of the day. Soon it was to become so obvious and dangerous a vice that legislation was introduced to check it. Not everyone was so sensible as Chesterfield who complained that at Bath he bored himself with low play, which he hated, in order to avoid high play which he loved. As we have seen, Nash did what he could to control gambling; it was in his interest to do so. At the same time he exerted his influence to prevent the foolish player from ruining himself at the tables and when this duly occurred (for his advice was rarely taken), he went to considerable lengths to help the victim. There are many stories of his generosity in this connection. Goldsmith tells of his behaviour towards a young earl who was bold enough to gamble against him. Predictably, the younger man lost steadily, for increasingly heavy stakes. Play went on until he had lost all his money, his family estate and even his carriage. No doubt pausing long enough to let him contemplate the extent of his ruin, Nash then flatly refused to take his winnings. Instead he asked for a promissory note of £5000, payable on demand. This note, in fact, he never presented, and the sum was eventually paid out of the earl's estate after his death. The shock, however, was enough to keep the loser away from the tables for the rest of his life.

Such stories bear a strong family resemblance to those of the kind-hearted prostitute, and it would be foolish to think that

Nash was entirely disinterested. Nevertheless, there was a streak of genuine good-heartedness in him, a remarkable characteristic in a man who, in general, was cynically preoccupied with his own interest. There are many stories of his generosity to those in need and they cannot all be dismissed as part of a thought-out policy of throwing bread upon the waters. Two examples will suffice: the weaving industry in the Bath area, once the major source of employment, had fallen on bad times, and when a crowd of starving weavers made their way into the city to beg for bread, it was Nash who came to their help. He gave them all an ample meal, and sent them off with a week's wages out of his own pocket. He seemed to find no inconsistency between such an act and his successful pressure on the city authorities in the same year to pass a byelaw by which beggars could be given a year's hard labour. Again, when the colliers in the Somerset coalfield fell out of work, he sponsored the raising of a subscription for them.

As a fund raiser, for good causes, Nash had in fact no equal. His special talent lay in taking money from the nobility, notoriously unwilling to part with funds which, having come to them as an inheritance, were plainly intended by Providence to be spent on themselves or passed on in turn to their heirs. His success is certainly to be attributed to the impudence of his attack, which was effective where a humbler approach would not have been. The well-known story of his victory over the thrifty Duchess of Marlborough is too good not to repeat. While engaged on his collection for the hospital, he found the duchess playing cards in the Assembly Rooms. In reply to his request for her support, she tried to fend him off by temporising. 'You must put me down for a trifle, Nash, but I have no money on me.' 'With pleasure, your Grace,' replied Nash, beginning to count guineas into his hand. 'If your Grace will tell me when to stop.' Before the duchess had understood what was happening the pile of coins was already a respectable size. Horrified, she begged him to stop. At 25 guineas he paused, but went on again. She managed in the end to halt him at 30 guineas. The duchess was almost speechless with fury. 'Stand further, you ugly devil,' she said, 'for I hate the sight of you.' And Nash went cheerfully away.

During the evening, the duchess had a run of good luck at the tables, made it up with Nash, and raised her contribution to 40 guineas, on the understanding that it should be anonymous. She had no intention of encouraging the belief that she was what would now be called a 'soft touch'.

The days when Nash himself could help the needy were numbered. There was a powerful puritan lobby in influential quarters. Having succeeded in closing the playhouses in 1736 it turned its attention to gambling and in 1739 an Act was passed making illegal the games of Faro, Basset, Hazard and Ace of Hearts—all the popular and, to Nash, profitable games. New games were, of course, immediately invented, only in their turn to be included in the schedule of illegal sports. All games 'with numbers thereon' became illegal and heavy fines were introduced to enforce the law. It requires no great wit to guess the next move in the game. Soon enough a new game, with letters substituted for figures, was devised in Tunbridge Wells. Nash saw its possibilities. First taking Counsel's Opinion, which confirmed its legality, he bought up all rights in the new game. 'E–O', as it was called (short for 'Even–Odd') was at once introduced at both spas, Nash taking a percentage of the profits. Unhappily his partners at both places seem to have cheated Nash systematically out of his share, and he sued them, claiming a sum of £20,000. It was an unwise step; not only did he not get his money, but he was suddenly revealed as having a vested interest in organised gambling. His amateur status was destroyed, and his social image irreparably tarnished. Then, in 1745, a new Act of Parliament, which made E–O illegal too, cut off the last main source of Nash's livelihood. Now a man of 71, he never recovered his prosperity or his reputation, and the remaining sixteen years of his life were passed in increasing penury and squalor. He had to give up his mansion in St John's Court and move to the smaller but still adequate house a few yards away which has retained his name. He appeared less and less at the Assembly Rooms, though when he did so he was still capable of dealing a sharp rebuke to conduct which did not conform to the standards he had set up nearly fifty years previously. But he was no longer treated with the same deference by the noble patrons; the duchesses, once

23 'E.O. or the Fashionable Vowels' from a cartoon by Thomas Rowlandson, 1781

proud to be noticed by him, turned their backs. In search of the homage which had become a necessity to him, he now frequented the inns, where among their casual customers he could still for a while hold court. Even here, however, the old Beau, now nearer 80 than 70, was eventually regarded as a bore, and became a butt for tavern wits.

In 1754, when he was 80, a subscription was opened on his behalf, nominally for a history of Bath and Tunbridge Wells and an autobiography which everyone knew he would never write. But this appeal was not the success that Nash's own appeals had been in earlier days; the touch of the old master was missing. A year before he died the authorities of the city, of whose fame and prosperity he was the main architect, awarded him the paltry pension of £10 a month. When in February 1761 he died at the age of 87, the same authorities gave him a civic funeral of considerable magnificence. There were high-flown obituary tributes in Latin and the vernacular which might have pleased him. And there was, in due course, a plaque in the Abbey. Juliana Papjoy had returned to nurse Nash in his last illness and now, her last service to her old lover rendered, she returned to her simpling and lived out the rest of her life in deranged silence, a homeless, harmless creature.

So Nash at last was dead. But his work had been well done and lived on. He had brought civility and order to an uncouth society, taught manners to the unmannerly and established a pattern of urbanity and good taste which stood for a century. It was not until it was called upon to bear the full weight of the vulgarity imposed on it by suddenly wealthy ironmasters and millowners in the mid-nineteenth century that it finally broke down.

VI

THE HEYDAY: 1705 to 1765

The heyday of Bath lasted rather more than a century, roughly from the arrival of Nash in 1705 to the end of the Regency in 1820. Over this long period the city and the life lived in it altered considerably, and it is convenient to make a rough dividing line at the decade which saw the deaths of the three creators of the city, John Wood in 1754, Nash in 1761 and Ralph Allen in 1764.

The social peak, measured simply in terms of the rank and wealth of the visitors, occurred at the very beginning of the period, in the first flush of Bath's fame as a resort of royalty and nobility. A high social plateau was then maintained until the second half of the century, when, with the growing popularity of the city, a decline set in. This decline, slight at first, became slowly steeper, until, by the time of Samuel Pickwick's famous visit in 1827, the glory had departed for ever.

Physically the trend is reversed: new building started slowly. Nothing much was done, as we have seen, before 1730, and the peak was not reached until about 1770. It is odd to think that Nash himself, who for most of us personifies Georgian Bath, died before it really existed, as Wood and Allen also did. When he died, Queen Square, the Circus and the Parades were already there in their first splendour; but the Royal Crescent, the new Assembly Rooms and Pulteney Bridge were still in the future. The upper town, Walcot, and the Bathwick estate had not been developed. The rage for new building reached its height in the last quarter of the century and was only halted by the economic and financial chaos that followed the French Revolution. One after another, the builders of the 1790s went bankrupt. By the early years of the new century, new building had practically ceased. In Chapter VII we shall look more closely at the architectural history of this period.

Over the period the cultural scene also changed considerably. Generally speaking the princes, courtiers and noblemen who first made Bath famous are themselves more notable for their ancestry and wealth than for their achievements or intrinsic interest. Their main historical function, looked at in retrospect, was to attract to Bath the artists, the entertainers, builders and tradesmen who would amuse, house and feed them. Their own main amusements, however, were simple and repetitive: card-playing and drinking, light chatter and philandering were generally enough. It was not until the gentry and the rich plebians had conquered a territory which was in the early days of the century still an exclusive resort for the nobility, that the cultural life of the city burst into full flower.

The theatre in the early days was closed as often as it was open and generally ill-patronised. There was little music. Those who, like Chesterfield, had intellectual or aesthetic tastes, got bored. After the anti-gaming laws of 1739–45, boredom must have become more general, until it was imperative to introduce other forms of entertainment. Little of interest emerges from these early years, except what is contained in letters from visitors who had a taste for correspondence: Chesterfield himself, and a number of gossips like Lady Suffolk. Steele's *Tatler* and *Guardian* confirm the vacuity of life at Bath at this period. He reports on the swarms of card-sharpers and doctors in the town—two doctors to each patient is his assessment—but finds little but irony for the cultural pursuits of the visitors. He satirises the idle versifiers who were already, it seems, a feature of the life of the place, and confers on them the title of 'Water Poets', by which their insipid successors two generations later were proud to be called. There were numerous painters in Bath at this period, miniaturists and portraitists, but their work was generally as mortal as their subjects, whose memorials cover the walls of the Abbey. No doubt, like the doctors, they throve, but we may wonder why in both cases.

It was in our second period, after the death of Nash and Allen, that Bath developed into the city which Landor compared with Florence. During the very time when the great nobility were beginning to stay away from Bath, the builders were creating a brilliant setting for their benefit. The lodgings designed for dukes were occupied instead by minor peers or mere gentlefolk. The courtiers stayed away, but their absence was more than made good by the less aristocratic but aesthetically more exacting and appreciative members of town and country society. What in modern terms could be called 'Bath's cultural explosion' was dramatic enough to require separate examination. Meanwhile, still in the earlier period, there was one place where interest in the arts and in artists flourished.

PRIOR PARK

Ralph Allen's house in Bath lay, it will be recalled, right in the middle of the quarter in which the social amenities of the city were concentrated. Within a few yards of the two Assembly Houses, it must have echoed constantly and intolerably to the traffic of visitors and the noise of the balls and entertainments. Allen decided to build himself a country house. Not only would this give him the peace which he could no longer find in Lilliput Alley, but also an opportunity to vindicate in a striking way the qualities of the stone from his quarries, which had recently been rejected by the London builders as unsuitable for the construction of Greenwich Hospital. Immediately to the east of the famous tramway which conveyed his stone from the Combe Down quarries to the river lay an area of steeply sloping ground forming the upper part of Widcombe valley. It was here at Prior Park that Allen decided to build his house. It was a superb site. From its high southern end, where the mansion would stand, the ground fell in a grand sweep towards the village of Widcombe and the river Avon. Across the river on the opposite slopes, the new city of Bath was beginning to rise, terrace by terrace, in the bright new stone from Allen's quarries. It was a fine view, and as each year more and more buildings went up, an increasingly

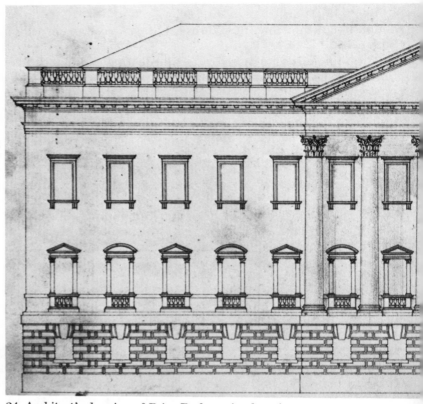

24 Architect's drawing of Prior Park, main elevation,
by John Wood the Elder

striking advertisement for the material of which they were made.
Thicknesse's superfluously ironic reference to Prior Park as a
'noble seat, which sees all Bath and which was built, probably, for
all Bath to see', precisely reflects Allen's intention.

John Wood was commissioned to build a house which, by its
grandeur of scale and delicacy of ornament, would demonstrate
once and for all the versatility of Bath stone. Wood's design
matched Allen's purpose. The great house, as he planned it, had
a frontage of 150 feet and was flanked by two pavilions housing

portes-cochères. Further out from the main house two symmetrical wings provided stabling, store-rooms and offices. A central pedimented portico, supported by giant Corinthian columns, occupied a third of the length and the whole height of the north front of the house, facing out over the valley. The effect as we still see it is totally magnificent. It was the finest house Wood had ever designed, and by far the finest for miles around. In the event only the mansion itself and the western range of buildings were built by Wood. Not for the first or last time the peppery architect quarrelled with his employer. For over ten years from 1735 he had been engaged on the work, but now it was handed over to Allen's Clerk of Works to complete. Wood's designs for the eastern range of buildings were altered for the worse. Allen himself aroused Wood's fury by introducing wooden wainscoting to replace the original stone adornment of the main rooms. Nothing, fortunately, was done to detract from the external splendour of the mansion itself. In the words of Ison, it remains 'one of the finest expressions of Palladian ideals and principles ever achieved in this country'. In 1755 a delightful addition was made at the lowest part of the estate, among the trees on the edge of the village of Widcombe. Here a Palladian bridge was built over a small lake. A fairly close copy of the bridge at Wilton, the seat of the Earls of Pembroke near Salisbury, it was a charming afterthought. Serving no particular purpose, it satisfied Allen's compulsive need to differentiate nature by the insertion of artificial features. But whereas Sham Castle, his earlier contribution of this kind, is in fact rather ridiculous, the bridge at Prior Park is completely successful. Against the trees and slopes behind, its pale stone and pure lines have the quality of a feature in a classical landscape.

Since 1829 Prior Park has been a Roman Catholic boys' school and is open at regular times to visitors. Although the flanking buildings have been altered unrecognisably—the two wings were reconstructed and heightened in the process and the west portico was demolished to make room for a fine church—the mansion itself, in spite of a disastrous fire which gutted it in 1836, remains essentially in its original state. Wood's grand design can be seen almost in its first glory. Inside the house the upper rooms have been considerably altered, but the ground floor is still as Wood planned it. His splendid chapel, a vaulted chamber two storeys high, has also survived with much of its original ornament. Bishop Baines, the founder of the college, deserves to be remembered, among other things, for an inspired addition in the grounds. He commissioned Goodridge, the Bath architect, to build an exterior stone staircase leading down from the great north front of the mansion; it fits in so well with the house itself that it might have been a part of the original design, and would

25 Prior Park—the North Portico

certainly have been approved by Allen, if not by Wood.

Allen moved to Prior Park before the whole scheme of building was complete, and from then until his death twenty years later kept open house to men of ability and distinction in many fields. Alexander Pope was so frequent and familiar a guest as almost to be admitted a member of the household, and Henry Fielding had his own regular place at Allen's table. Gainsborough, who began his career in Bath, and Hoare, the Bath portrait-painter, were frequent guests. So too was James Quin the actor. Samuel Richardson, the novelist, was a visitor, and David Garrick, friend of Dr Johnson and the leading actor of his time, was a close friend, and for years kept up a regular correspondence with his generous host.

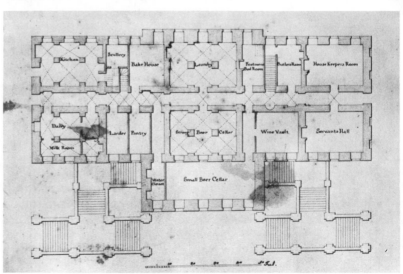

90

26 (*left*) Prior Park (built by John Wood the Elder, 1735–48)

27 (*below, left*) Architect's drawing of Prior Park,
basement plan, by John Wood the Elder

28 (*below*) The Palladian Bridge, Prior Park, c. 1755

Of all Allen's guests, Quin was among the most entertaining and certainly the oddest. The last great exponent of the declamatory school of acting, he retired to Bath in 1751, and devoted the remaining fifteen years of his life to the enjoyment of his favourite pleasures. A famous wit, gourmand and toper, it is not surprising that his most notable stage-part had been that of Falstaff, whom he resembled closely in character, tastes and not least in size; Quin was enormous. He appears under his own name in Smollett's *Humphrey Clinker*, where his Gargantuan appetite for wine and good food is frankly but amiably recorded. Smollett describes how Quin, after dining on a Friday at the Three Tuns, a coaching inn in Stall Street where he had his own table, is carried home with 'six good bottles of claret under his belt', having given orders not to be disturbed until noon on the following Sunday. His conversation, it appears, was totally unaffected by the wine which had taken the use of his legs, and was as humorous and incisive as ever. Such a character would have been a welcome guest at Prior Park, where good talk was appreciated and a couch was always at the disposal of visitors temporarily overcome by hospitality.

*   *   *

Allen had a special kindness for writers and gave them generous hospitality and financial aid when they needed it. Both Henry Fielding, and his sister Sarah, also a novelist, were helped in this way. Fielding, who lived at Twerton, on the outskirts of Bath, while he was writing *Tom Jones*, dined daily it is said at Prior Park, while his sister seems to have received a pension of £100 in return for the pleasure her writing gave to Allen. In *Tom Jones* Squire Allworthy is explicitly modelled on Allen, for whom Fielding had unlimited admiration. He was also, unlike some artists in their relations with their patrons, grateful for the generosity he received. He praises Allen for his hospitality, stressing that he did not require in return that his guests should entertain him; they were, on the contrary 'perfect masters of their time'. Part of the character sketch given in the novel is worth quoting, since it reflects the almost universal esteem in

29 James Quin, by William Hogarth

which Allen was held by those who knew him. Fielding writes that he

had known a man whose penetrating genius had enabled him to raise a large fortune in a way where no beginning was chaulked out to him; that he had done this with the most perfect preservation of his integrity, and not only without the least injustice or injury to any one individual person, but with the highest advantage to trade, and a vast increase of the public revenue; . . . that he was most industrious in searching after merit in distress, most eager to relieve it, and then as careful (perhaps too careful) to conceal what he had done.

He described Allen as 'a munificent patron, a warm and firm friend . . . hospitable to his neighbours, charitable to the poor, and benevolent to all mankind'. 'This was the only house in the kingdom,' he said, referring to what must be Prior Park, 'where you was sure to gain a dinner by deserving it.'

Of all the literary friendships based on Allen's hospitality and charm of character, that with Alexander Pope is the best known. Pope's first recorded visit to Bath had been in 1714, when, writing to his lifelong friends the Blount sisters, he was critical of Nash, but asserted that Bath had 'the finest promenades in the world'. He continued to frequent the city and now, more than twenty years later, the publication of his letters had attracted Allen's admiration and led him to seek acquaintance with the poet. Although Pope vehemently condemned the 'unauthorised' publication of these letters, it is clear enough that he had in fact engineered it, and indeed had written with publication in view. It is in keeping with Allen's innocence of mind that he never seems to have suspected the truth and indeed offered to finance the subsequent issue of an 'authorised' edition. At all events the friendship between the two quickly ripened, and Pope soon became 'almost a constant inmate of the family during the Bath season for many years'. His regard for his host is expressed in a famous reference in the epilogue to his Satires:

> *Let humble Allen, with an awkward shame,*
> *Do good by stealth and blush to find it fame.*

If in the first version of these lines, the author wrote 'low born' instead of 'humble', at least he had the grace to make the alteration, characteristically not at Allen's request. In 1741, Pope wrote pressingly to his friend Warburton, inviting him to make a lengthy stay at Prior Park, describing his host as 'sincere and plainer than almost any man in the world'. The invitation was accepted, and Warburton, a witty and attractive cleric, notorious however for his quarrelsome nature, became as much a member of the household as Pope, more so in fact, since in 1745 he married Allen's niece and made his home henceforth at Prior Park. It was largely by Allen's influence with Pitt that Warburton became Dean of Bristol and later Bishop of Gloucester; and, on Allen's death, he effectively inherited the great house in which he had so long been a non-paying guest and which was now bequeathed to his wife.

Meanwhile Pope, on his annual visits to Bath, generally stayed with Allen, where he could be sure of finding not only a warm welcome from his host but cultured and amusing company. All went well until in 1743 he brought Martha Blount with him. It seems likely that the Allens, particularly Mrs Allen, neither liked the lady nor approved of the intimacy of her relationship with the poet, and at times did not exert themselves to conceal their feelings. In due course there was a disagreement of some magnitude, followed by a scene in which Warburton sided with the Allens. Pope at once left the house, leaving the wretched Martha, who for some reason could not accompany him, alone and unsupported until she too could make her departure. The breach was a serious one, though the cause of it cannot have been a matter of any great importance. Although by the following January, Allen and Pope were again in friendly correspondence, an 'explication' was apparently called for, and Allen visited the poet in London in March for this purpose. Allen denied any intended unfriendliness on his side, and put the whole thing down to a misunderstanding between the ladies. Peace appeared to be restored, but the final word in the matter, a wounding and malicious one, was held in reserve by Pope. On his death, only a few weeks later, his will was found to include a legacy of £150 to Allen 'being to the best of my calculation the amount of what I have received from him'. Allen, before handing this paltry sum over to charity, said, rather wrily, that £1500 would have been a nearer assessment of the debt which the will purported to discharge. It was a poor postscript to the story of a long friendship.

In 1742, Allen had been elected Mayor of Bath and had acquired an ascendancy in the affairs of the city which increased year by year; so much so that the city fathers were to receive the contemptuous label of 'The One-Headed Corporation'. He was on all counts the outstanding citizen of Bath. Not only was he the wealthiest, but his control of the postal services and his ownership of the stone quarries gave him a position of unique power in the economic life of the city. Moreover his father-in-law, General Wade, was the Member for Bath from 1722 until his death in 1748, and through him Allen had access to political circles in London, an invaluable qualification in a leader of local government.

It was certainly Allen who was instrumental in obtaining the services of Pitt as Bath's Member of Parliament in 1757. The two had met three years before, when Pitt was in Bath suffering from illness, and Allen had taken the leading part in a demonstration organised by the city in Pitt's honour. As Member for Bath, Pitt was at the head of a ministry whose main concern was the conduct of the Seven Years' War, the war which, through Pitt's skilful strategy, drove the French out of India and Canada, and established British dominion in these great territories. Forced to resign in 1761, Pitt bitterly opposed the draft terms of the Treaty of Paris, which in his view provided too little return for Britain's investment in the struggle. In a famous speech, he was scornfully critical of the proposed peace on these grounds. It was therefore extremely tactless of the Corporation, when the Treaty was nevertheless signed in 1763, to send a congratulatory address to the king on the event, particularly since it would be Pitt's duty, as the city's representative, to transmit it to the Crown. When he found that the address described the terms of the peace as 'adequate' (he had constantly used the word 'inadequate' in the same context) he can be forgiven for thinking that the document was a deliberate personal affront. He refused to forward it, and there was an open breach between him and his constituents. Allen, who in fact agreed with the Corporation in their views on the peace, tried in vain to heal the breach. Pitt sold his house in the Circus and did not visit Bath again in his official capacity, although he continued as its Member until, in 1766, he was made Earl of Chatham. Personal relations between Pitt and Allen remained cordial throughout, and Allen left £1000 to the statesman in his will, with an appropriate message of esteem.

The contrast between the brilliance of the society to be found at Prior Park with its artists and writers, and the dullness of Bath itself, with its noble visitors bowed over the gambling tables, is striking. The difference between the characters of Allen and Nash is equally marked; both created for themselves the world they wanted. Perhaps it is ironic that, whereas Allen's world died with him (he even had no direct heir to live in his great house) Nash, trivial as his tastes and outlook were, had launched a society which was to reach its highest point only after his death.

A visitor to Bath in the early or middle years of the century would have been entitled to think, as he was jostled by an earl in the Pump Room or made way for a duchess on the Grand Parade, that the spa was then at the height of its brilliance. He would have been right only in the sense that Bath would never again be so 'smart', nor its visitors' book so full of aristocratic names. By every other standard the great days were still to come. None of the three founding fathers lived long enough to see the city which was their creation reach the summit of its glory. Within ten years of each other, they were all dead. The next generation would show how well their work had been done.

VII

'THE RAGE OF BUILDING'

THE LATER ARCHITECTS

The population of Bath when Nash arrived there was some 2000. At his death it was 10,000 and by 1800 it had risen to 34,000. John Wood's contribution to the task of providing accommodation for the hordes of visitors clamouring for lodging was massive but was little more than a beginning. Much more remained to be done than he had managed to achieve. His great rôle had been to set a pattern for his successors to follow. He set a magnificent example. His work was never to be surpassed, except on an inspired occasion by his son. But it had to be continued without delay. It is the work of those who completed what Wood had begun that we are now concerned with.

It is a remarkable fact that Georgian Bath is almost entirely the work of local men. Only Robert Adam was truly a 'foreigner' and he is represented in Bath only by Pulteney Bridge. Strahan admittedly had made a name in Bristol before working in Bath, and John Wood did important work in other parts of the country. But the others were craftsmen who had learned their trade in the city itself and did little if any work elsewhere. Nor were they architects in the modern sense. In the days before formal professional training, as distinct from craft apprenticeship, existed, the very word architect was rarely used. When it was, it indicated a man who had studied classical Italian buildings on the spot and understood the ancient Roman principles of construction and ornament, or who had made an academic study of them in the works of Vitruvius and his commentator Palladio. John Wood fell into the second, much larger, category, and had worked under the leaders of the classical revival before coming to Bath.

His successors were not so. They were practical builders, who had begun their careers as plumbers, painters, masons, joiners or surveyors, and had then set up as independent contractors. Some had turned to building from other less profitable callings. In this they were not exceptional; Christopher Wren himself was over forty when he turned from astronomy to architecture. What was exceptional was the opportunity offered by the needs of Bath. There were fortunes to be made. The demand was clamorous and plentiful supplies of stone were cheaply available on the spot. All that was needed was the ability to build attractively in the classical style which was alone acceptable. Guidance was readily available. Wren had produced in the previous century standardised and simplified designs which enabled small builders to duplicate his manner without difficulty. Colin Campbell had now published his *Vitruvius Britannicus* and a host of 'pattern-books' followed. As long as a builder did not depart from the designs he found in them he could produce a passable version of the style which everyone wanted. Originality was not asked for and was indeed positively discouraged. These facts—the existence of comprehensive text-books and the demand for rigid conformity with 'classical' rules of design and ornament—made Georgian architecture possible.[1] They are perhaps too easily taken to provide all the explanation needed for the splendid achievements of the builders of Bath. I cannot think that this is so. It seems to me nearer the truth to say that John Wood's work was both a model and a challenge to those who had to put their work next to his, where it would be compared in general and in

---

[1] The consummate skill of the later Georgian designers could not have been learned wholly from 'pattern-books'. In nearly all of their work still remaining there is great understanding of the subtleties of the proportions of solids and voids. Their ingenuity is also shown in the many terraces so naturally rising across the contours of steeply sloping hillsides.

particular with the great creations of the old master. Building which would always be seen alongside his masterpieces had to be good. And so primarily it was.

We have now seen how, on Wood's death, the Circus he had designed was still to be built, and that it was his son, John Wood the Younger, who took up and completed the work. Unable to foresee the tremendous demand for housing that would have to be met within a few years of his death, the elder Wood had planned to close off his Circus by two short streets running east and west, each terminated by a suitably noble building. Instead of this the whole area surrounding the Circus was to be built over within twenty years and linked to the Lower Town by new thoroughfares. If in this hectic period of building the speculative builders who carried out the work had done so piecemeal, in the way of their kind, each ignoring the work of their competitors, the result could have been calamitous. In fact the whole area from Marlborough Buildings in the west to Belmont in the east and as far north as Julian Road has a harmony of design which can only be explained by the existence of a master-plan. There is every reason on stylistic grounds to conclude, as Ison does, that it was John Wood the Younger who produced this plan.

Certainly Wood's position as an architect was by this time beyond challenge, for he had already created two masterpieces, the Royal Crescent and the New Assembly Rooms; to the west and east respectively of his father's Circus. It is the former which establishes the younger Wood as an architect of genius. Not only is it, in a city of fine streets and buildings, easily the most glorious creation, but it has no equal in the whole of England. In the words of Ison, a sober and expert judge, it is 'the greatest single achievement in the whole field of our urban architecture'. Instead of the short street intended by his father at the western exit of the Circus, Wood designed a much longer one, providing access to a superb site high above an open expanse of sloping fields to the south. In 1767 work was begun both on Brock Street and the Crescent. Brock Street was designed by Wood in a sober style, with the clear intention of supplying an interval of repose between the splendours of the two great creations at each end. Today only the north side between Margaret's Buildings and the

30 The Royal Crescent from the south-east, from a
drawing by Thomas Malton the Younger, 1784

Crescent remains relatively free from later alteration. In the
centre of this block is the entrance to what was the Margaret
Chapel, a proprietary chapel designed by Wood for the benefit of
the residents of the new quarter. The chapel itself, named after
the then Lady of the Manor, was an unsatisfactory excursion
into pseudo-Gothic. It fell into disuse and after a long period of
miscellaneous and increasingly undignified employment was
finally destroyed in the air-raids of 1942. All that now remains of
interest is the fine first-storey window in the house over the
entrance to the chapel.

The Royal Crescent was eight years in building. It is the work
of many hands, small groups of building craftsmen joining forces
to erect individual houses, but all in strict conformity with
Wood's design for their exterior. The design comprises a great
curve of 30 houses of identical pattern, almost 50 feet high
and over 500 feet in length. The ground-floor storey is severely
simple and for the balustrade which surmounts the frontage

101

31 The Royal Crescent (built by
John Wood the Younger, 1767–75)

Wood dispensed with the adornments which his father had employed in a similar position in the Circus frontage, contenting himself with the simplest arrangement of plain dies and balusters. The simplicity of these sections of the building was well conceived by Wood to heighten the drama of the main feature of the Crescent, the giant order of 114 columns, over twenty feet high, which are attached to the first and second storeys. The end-pavilions and the central house of the Crescent are marked by paired columns and the latter has a round-headed window; there is no other feature to vary the splendid uniformity of the elevation.

A catalogue of characteristics and statistics can no more give a picture of the Crescent than an anatomical inventory can recreate a Botticellian Venus. It must be seen, preferably on a sunlit day, with enough cloud to give contrasting light. It should be viewed first from the Brock Street end, where the visitor emerges from a tranquil stretch of undramatic houses onto a superb platform on which sky and stone meet in a moment of unique harmony and drama. To the left the ground falls away in sloping lawns to the Lower Town and the hidden river. Trees rise over the skyline. To the right, beyond the original cobbled roadway and the wide pavement, an unbroken sweep of lovely stone, pillared and corniced, rises in calm splendour. It is impossible not to be astonished at one's first sight, and familiarity breeds only increasing delight. The Royal Crescent is the climax of Bath architecture; there is nothing finer.

The tall houses are now largely turned into flats. Modern servants, even if they were available, would not tolerate the conditions under which Wood's builders arranged for them to live. Their bedrooms at the top of the house are cramped and tiny; and there are too many stairs. With admirable enterprise, the Bath Preservation Trust has, while this book was being prepared, taken over the first house at the Brock Street end of the Crescent and is providing it with contemporary furniture and fittings. Here the present-day visitor may gain a unique impression of an eighteenth-century Bath lodging.

From the time of the completion of the Circus it became increasingly clear that it was in the area surrounding it that the city would expand. By 1763 Milsom Street existed, providing access to the land north of George Street, where the map would soon fill with plans for building. In a few years all the southern slopes of Lansdown would be built over. It became urgent to think of an entertainment centre for visitors who would be pleased neither by their unmodish remoteness from the hub of social life which was still in the region of the Abbey, nor by the expense and discomfort of constant journeys up and downhill by chair. Of the two Assembly Rooms, Wiltshire's was already too small, and the balls at Simpson's were also becoming uncomfortably crowded. To provide for the new population of the Upper Town a more commodious and accessible building was needed. An enterprising group of residents therefore banded together into a tontine[1] for the purpose, under the watchful eye of John Wood, in whose house in Brock Street the shareholders met. The first proposed site fell through, and Wood quickly built Queen's Parade on it. Robert Adam was then invited to submit designs for a building on what was to be the eventual site, but they were too expensive and ambitious, and Wood's own scheme, on similar but less splendid lines, was finally accepted. Building began in 1769 and was completed two years later at an inclusive cost of £20,000.

The New or Upper Rooms, as they were called, were an immediate success. Wiltshire's Rooms, already struggling desperately to hold their place in competition with Simpson's, closed their doors almost immediately and for good. Even Simpson's, now called the Lower Rooms, had a hard time to compete with the splendour of their new rival. In order to achieve a balance and to share the entertainment programme out fairly between the two establishments, two Masters of Ceremonies were now appointed, one for each set of Rooms. It was an arrangement which incorporated its own problems, and introduced conflict as well as competition. The Lower Rooms never regained their former

---

[1] A tontine was a system of raising a loan, much used at the time, by which, as each subscriber died, the share of interest or annuity received by the survivors increased proportionately, until the last survivor inherited all. One can imagine the tension that built up among the heirs as the last two members of a tontine clung stubbornly to life.

popularity, although they continued to offer a programme of entertainment for many years. In 1820, a disastrous fire closed them
for good. The New Rooms went from strength to strength. Even
when Bath was no longer a fashionable spa they continued to
thrive. Throughout the nineteenth century concerts and exhibi-
tions kept the Assembly Rooms, as they were now quite simply
called, the centre of the city's entertainment. Johann Strauss and
Liszt performed there and later Madame Patti, Rubinstein and
Pachmann. Charles Dickens gave his famous public readings
there. Not till the early twentieth century did the fortunes of the
Rooms decline. The ballroom became successively a cinema, a
tea-room and a sale-room. In 1931 the building was acquired
through a private benefactor by the National Trust and leased
to the city, who undertook to carry out a complete restoration.
This work was faithfully done by Mowbray Green, the leading
authority of the day on the eighteenth-century architecture of
Bath, and a year before the outbreak of the Second World War,
the Rooms were once more formally opened. In the air-raids of
1942 the Rooms were almost completely gutted by incendiary
bombs and they remained derelict until 1957, when the National

32 The Assembly Rooms: main entrance and forecourt
(built by John Wood the Younger, 1768–71)

Trust undertook a second restoration. The whole building was once more laboriously restored to its original form by the late Sir Albert Richardson, with a new décor by Oliver Messel, in strict keeping with late eighteenth-century taste. The magnificent chandeliers, removed for safety during the war, were replaced in their original position, and in 1963 the Rooms were re-opened, in something very near to their first splendour.

The general layout of the New Assembly Rooms as planned by Wood resembles the earlier plan of Robert Adam, consisting of a ballroom, a tea-room and a concert-room or card-room, arranged round a central ante-room, but with much simplified decoration. The building is approximately square in plan, with its main entrance to the west opening on to a wide paved area, where the sedan chairmen could deposit their fares without excessive jostling. The carriage-entrances were in Alfred Street and Bennett Street. The absence of external windows in the upper part of the north and west walls gives a rather forbidding air to these frontages, and it is the Alfred Street front which is the most effective, with its fine and well-balanced arrangement of windows. Inside the building, the central ante-room is a

charmingly decorated octagon, from which there is access to the three main rooms; the ballroom to the left, the tea-room to the right and the octagonal card-room straight ahead. The ballroom, over a hundred feet long, is oblong, with tall Corinthian columns and pilasters and a high coved ceiling, from which hang five superb chandeliers. There is a lofty semi-circular recess for the musicians. The card-room has a musicians' gallery, four marble fireplaces and a fine central chandelier, while the walls contain frames designed for portraits. In keeping with the tradition of Nash's day, a portrait by Gainsborough of Captain Wade, Master of Ceremonies when the Rooms were opened, was hung in this room and remained there until the early years of the present century, when the owners of the Rooms, a private company, were forced by financial necessity to sell it, along with other portraits and much of the furnishings. (This event occurred during the tenure of office of the last Master of Ceremonies, a Major Simpson. On his death in 1914 the appointment finally lapsed.)

The main feature of the tea-room is the two-storeyed colonnade at its west end, in the upper section of which the musicians sat.

33 The Assembly Rooms, Alfred Street frontage, drawing by Thomas Malton, c. 1777

34 The Assembly Rooms, ballroom

An order of Corinthian columns, as in the ballroom, surrounds the room at this level, immediately below the coved ceiling, with its three original chandeliers. In 1777 an additional card-room of more modest design was added to the east of the original octagon. Only parts of the tea-room survived the air-raid of 1942, but the restoration of the Rooms as a whole has been extremely well carried out, and it is here as much as in the Pump Room that one gains an impression of the splendid setting in which the life of Bath went on in the last quarter of the eighteenth century, the true heyday of the spa.

In 1767 Wood the Younger's men had laid the first stones of Brock Street; ten years later the whole Upper Town as far north

35 The Assembly Rooms, tea-room

as Julian Road was complete. It was a decade of astonishing achievement both in quality and quantity. The Royal Crescent, the Assembly Rooms and half a dozen streets of impeccable design, were all built in this brief period. It is extraordinary to think that the sole designer of what is undoubtedly the finest group of streets and buildings in Bath has been regarded by many as merely the respectably gifted son of a brilliant father. There can surely be no disagreement with Ison's opinion that 'the finest achievements of the son surpass those of the father, both in breadth of conception and subtlety of realisation'. While the New Town was rising at this tremendous pace, the city fathers were busy on another project elsewhere. It was, one might have thought, a relatively simple one. The Guildhall, built in the previous century to a design said to have been by Inigo Jones, stood in the Market Place, which occupied the area at the lower end of the present High Street, between the Orange Grove and the eastern end of Cheap Street ('cheap' of course means market). It was acknowledged to be too small and, on its island site in a

110

congested area, an intolerable obstruction through which visitors whether on foot or in chairs could barely force a way. In 1763, after several years of discussion, the Common Council took the time-honoured first step in municipal affairs: it set up a committee, with the task of making proposals for the erection of a new Guildhall in a less inconvenient spot. The committee and its successors sat for thirteen years and in turn considered six designs by five different architects before the first stone of the new building was laid in 1776.

It is an extraordinary story of vacillation and intrigue, behind-the-scene jobbery over contracts and acrimonious public controversy. The central figure in this involved tale is Thomas Atwood, who was a leading member of the Building Committee as well as holding the appointment of City Surveyor. He was thus able, as a councillor, to steer building policy in directions which gave him, as official architect, endless opportunities to acquire profitable contracts. Not only was it his function to build for the Corporation, but his position enabled him to obtain leases of city property and develop them in a private capacity. By this method he built the Paragon and Oxford Row on the west side of Lansdown Road. Fortunately he was a sound architect and the Paragon is a fine sweep of well-designed houses. The new prison which he built for the Corporation across the river in Bathwick, in what is now Grove Street, has also an excellently designed Palladian frontage in an appropriately heavy idiom. The first design for the new Guildhall was by Thomas Lightoler, then also occupied with plans for the Octagon Chapel. A second, more modest plan was then invited, and Lightoler revised his designs for the Guildhall while Wood, assisted by Jones, Ralph Allen's former Clerk of Works, produced ground-plans for the market and Guildhall area. In the following year a third plan was produced and, in 1768 the Mayor laid the foundation-stone. This was a premature step. Tenders were not called for for another five years, and two years after that (in 1775) it was a new plan by Atwood which received the Corporation's approval. It is perhaps not unfair to deduce that Atwood had been for ten years quietly sabotaging his competitors' efforts until in the end he got the job.

The climax to this rather unedifying tale, however, was yet to

come. John Palmer, later the architect of Lansdown Crescent,
but at this stage merely Thomas Jelly's junior partner, produced,
uninvited, a new plan, the fifth in the series, which had great
merit on the score of economy, and to which Jelly was prepared
to work without a cash payment, in return for a long lease of
the market buildings. The Corporation, already committed to
Atwood, to whose design building had actually started, barely
looked at Palmer's plan before rejecting it. There was now an
immediate and vociferous attack on the Corporation in the local
press, with Atwood and his jobbery as the main target. Atwood's
single contribution to the debate was a technical criticism of
Palmer's plan; this fell flat when it was shown to be based on a
serious miscalculation in Atwood's own plan. The wrangle was
only terminated by Atwood's death in the same year as the result
of an accident, when the floor of an old house in the market
place collapsed on him. This event allowed the Corporation,
without loss of face, to call in a new architect. Their choice fell
on Thomas Baldwin, Atwood's former assistant, a young man
of 25, whose plans were accepted by the city in the year

38 Somersetshire Buildings in Milsom Street, built by Thomas Baldwin,
1781–83, drawing by Thomas Malton the Younger, 1784

after Atwood's death. Now at long last building could effectively
begin. In the time which had elapsed since the original decision
to build the new Guildhall, Wood had designed the Royal
Crescent and the Assembly Rooms and they and the surrounding
network of streets had been built. If there is a moral in all this, it
will not comfort the advocates of municipal enterprise.

The Guildhall finally built to Baldwin's design was an excellent
building. Seen from the High Street, only the central section of
the frontage is original, the flanking wings having been added in

114

1893 by Brydon, a competent designer whose additions to the building, which include the shallow dome surmounting it, are as acceptable as architectural afterthoughts can be expected to be. The rear elevation of Baldwin's building, somewhat obscured by later building, is as fine in its way as the main frontage. Both would have shocked the elder Wood and his disciples, since the ornamental features of their style—vases, oval windows and festoons—depart markedly from the true Palladian pattern. Baldwin was an early follower of the Adam brothers, whose publication *Works in Architecture* was published in instalments from 1773 and gave a new direction to English domestic architecture. Their free treatment of classical conventions, and particularly their imaginative use of ornament to lighten the severity of the earlier style, was refreshing and timely. Baldwin, in the Guildhall and his later work, showed himself a brilliant exponent of their manner. His great achievement in the Guildhall is the Banqueting Hall. To those familiar with the dreary interiors of most town halls this magnificent room will be totally unexpected. Ison did no more than express the general opinion when he called it 'beyond any question the finest interior in Bath, and a masterpiece of late eighteenth-century decoration'. Eighty feet long and superbly proportioned, its walls and ceiling have a richness and variety not previously seen in Bath and never later surpassed. Frieze, cornice, architrave and lunettes are adorned with delicate moulding and ornament in such profusion that only their lightness of design and execution prevents a sense of excess. The three great chandeliers are as fine as, if not finer than, those in the Assembly Rooms. It can almost be said that this marvellous room is a composition in the musical sense, each ornamental feature contributing to the harmony of the whole, like the themes in a symphony.

Baldwin was appointed City Surveyor in the year when he designed the Guildhall; he was to have a brilliant future as an architect both in a civic and a private capacity. His first notable achievement in the latter field was the designing in 1782 of Somersetshire Buildings on the east side of Milsom Street, on the vacant site of the old Poor House. This group of five houses, with its pillared and pedimented end-pavilions and the bow-fronted central house, dominates the whole street. Although modern shop-fronts now mar the design, the upper storeys retain their original excellence. Milsom Street had been constructed in 1763. It is named after Daniel Milsom, a wine-cooper who leased from the Corporation the land on which it stands, known then as Milsom's Garden, and also the Town Acre, the site of the present Edgar Buildings. Building on both sites was conducted as a joint venture by the Corporation and Milsom, and the houses have Palladian frontages of the type standard at the time for buildings on Corporation property. Edgar Buildings was designed as a single terrace-unit, with a pedimented central house, effectively sited to close off the vista from Milsom Street.

Just below Somersetshire Buildings is an easily overlooked entrance giving access to what was in its day the most famous of Bath's proprietary chapels, the Octagon. These chapels, of which there were six in all, were built (as their name implies) by private speculators, whose object was as much their own profit as the spiritual welfare of those who, on payment of substantial pew-rents, had the privilege of worshipping in them. Their history begins in London, where the Mayfair Chapel in Curzon Street was erected in 1730 to serve the newly fashionable quarter north of Piccadilly. Although not consecrated, and thus not able to offer Holy Communion, the Mayfair Chapel and the other proprietary chapels which soon came into existence were entitled to perform 'Fleet marriages', for which no licence, banns or parental consent were required. Such marriages were both perfectly legal and extremely profitable to those who performed them. Thus Dr Alexander Keith, the incumbent of the Mayfair Chapel, made what Horace Walpole called 'a bishopric of a revenue', performing in one year 700 marriages at a guinea each, whereas at the regular parish church only forty were solemnised in the same period. While the Bath chapels did little trade in marriages, they made a good income from pew-rents, and could afford to offer powerful attractions by way of exciting preachers and good music. (Herschel, as we shall shortly see, was for a time organist at the Octagon.) The first chapel of the kind in Bath was St Mary's Chapel, already referred to, put up in 1734 by the elder John Wood for the tenants of Queen Square. This was followed by five other chapels strategically sited for the convenience of the new housing areas of Lansdown, Bathwick, Walcot, the Crescent and Milsom Street. Of them all only two have survived, and neither is in use for its original purpose. The Kensington Chapel on the London Road, with its excellent frontage designed by Palmer, is used as a warehouse, while the Octagon is used for a variety of purposes as a display-room.

Unlike the Kensington Chapel, whose interior has been stripped, the Octagon has largely retained its original structure and ornament. The octagonal shape of the chapel is extended by semi-circular alcoves, in two of which are fireplaces, and by the sanctuary on the east wall. Galleried and domed, with its walls richly decorated, and an altar-piece by William Hoare, the Bath Academician, it was a temple of great elegance, and a profitable investment for its owners.

While the Milsom Street area was being developed, a great project was afoot across the river at Bathwick. The Bathwick estate, owned by Sir William Pulteney, was excellently sited for building purposes, except for the fact that access to the city depended on the ferry serving Spring Gardens. As a first step in the development of the estate for housing it was plainly necessary to replace this ferry by a road-bridge. Pulteney was a friend of Robert Adam and commissioned him to design first the bridge and then the streets and houses of the proposed building scheme. In the event Pulteney died before his major project could be launched. Only the famous bridge, named for him, was built in his lifetime. It is the only example of Adam's work in the city; it is also unique in being the only city bridge in Britain which is built over from end to end. It is a lovely creation as well as a unique one; even in its present state, with its design marred by later alterations and its beauty vitiated by the clutter of modern shop-windows, it keeps its grace and charm. The tall Venetian windows which are the dominant central feature are balanced by domed pavilions at each end, originally set off by free-standing columns. The roof-line has been raised and a row of mean windows inserted, thus spoiling the effect of Adam's original design, in which pyramidally-roofed pavilions above the mid-stream piers broke the skyline and were linked with the central

117

39 Pulteney Bridge from the Grand Parade,
built by Robert Adam, 1769–74

feature by a balustrade. It is to be hoped that a major restoration may be possible and that this fine Adam design may once more be seen in something like its original form.

The bridge took five years, from 1769 to 1774, to build. Adam's plans for the estate were then prepared. His first scheme linked the bridge by a wide road to a great circus from which five other streets led off. These in turn were crossed by streets converging on a semi-circular open space at the bridge-entrance. It was a fine, ambitious but costly scheme. A second scheme of much less merit was later made by Adam but his patron died before either could be realised. Pulteney's daughter Henrietta, acting perhaps under local pressure, now turned to Baldwin and he produced the plan which was finally adopted. His scheme incorporated Adam's conception of a wide street leading from the bridge across the estate, but omitted the semi-circular area in front of the bridge and rejected Adam's circus, the focal point of the original design. Work began on Baldwin's plans in 1788. Argyle Street, Laura Place, Henrietta Street and Great Pulteney Street itself were soon built. At this stage the nation-wide financial panic caused by the French Revolution forced the collapse of many banks, including the one which largely provided the funds for the Bathwick undertaking. One by one the builders, including Eveleigh and Baldwin himself, went into bankruptcy and all work stopped. At the far end of Great Pulteney Street Baldwin had planned the layout of a large hexagonal pleasure garden, surrounded by eight terraces of houses, with an hotel facing up the wide street towards the city. Of this ambitious project he was able to complete only one terrace of what became Sydney Place before ruin overtook him. Harcourt Masters took over the scheme and Sydney Gardens with its Vauxhall became an immensely popular place of resort. The Sydney Hotel, redesigned by Masters much on the lines of Baldwin's plan, forms, with its pedimented portico, and tall Corinthian columns, a fitting terminal to Great Pulteney Street. Today, much altered from its original form, it houses the Holburne of Menstrie Museum.

Baldwin's plans for the Bathwick estate show him to have been a town planner of extraordinary vision and skill. Great Pulteney Street, over 1000 feet long and 100 feet wide, is easily the finest street in Bath and among the most impressive in England. Seen from Laura Place, its long vista closed by the pillared front of the museum and the trees of Sydney Gardens, it is magnificent. It was to provide, in the next century, a fitting home for the exiled French monarchy and its entourage. Criticism could possibly be made of its architectural detail, but this will not trouble the general visitor and does not reduce the overall effect of spaciousness and dignity. One must however regret that Baldwin rejected Adam's plan for an open area at the Pulteney Bridge end; Argyle Street is a mean alternative, and it may be that Baldwin's plans were not in fact faithfully carried out here. The early shop-fronts on its south side are nevertheless charming.

For Baldwin the period from 1776, when his designs for the Guildhall were accepted, to his bankruptcy in 1793 was one of

40 Laura Place

121

41 Great Pulteney Street from Laura Place

fantastic activity. Not only was he engaged in work as a private
architect and builder, but he was the City Surveyor during the
whole of this time. In the latter capacity he was commissioned
to carry out major improvements at the bathing establishment.
This involved nothing less than the rebuilding of the Cross Bath,
the provision of new private baths, the reconstruction of the
Pump Room and indeed the redesigning of the whole area
occupied by the baths and the street giving access to them. His
plans for this complex and important work were approved in
1788, the very year in which he began the development of Bathwick. No wonder that he had to neglect his personal affairs and
thus hasten his own ruin five years later. The Corporation's
decision to carry out a comprehensive rebuilding plan at the

122

bathing establishment was long overdue. Not only were the baths themselves in great need of modernisation, but the street and buildings around them were dingy and tumbledown, in scandalous contrast with the splendour of the new town. As long ago as 1749 the elder Wood claimed to have 'kept this Matter under Consideration for more than thrice seven Years', but his plans were too typically grandiose and they were shelved. The 'open, unseemly ponds' described in 1763 by Dr Sutherland, with their incrusted walls 'exposed to wind and rain, as well as to the gaping of every footman', remained much as they were. The baths built by the Duke of Kingston as a private venture in 1766 on the site of the old Abbey House were much more elegant and convenient than those owned by the city, and attracted all those who were ready to pay five shillings for their use. (These baths stood over the eastern range of the Roman baths and used water supplied by a Roman culvert. During their construction the Roman 'Lucas bath' was discovered but no further excavation was made. The Kingston baths were demolished when the Roman baths were excavated at the end of the nineteenth

42 The Pump Room and colonnade from the corner of
Bath Street, from a drawing by Spornberg, 1801

century.) Stimulated into action perhaps by this competition, the Corporation gave the younger Wood his only civic commission, to reconstruct the Hot Bath, in 1775. He designed an octagonal bath, open to the sky, surrounded by an array of small baths and dressing-rooms, still in use as part of the medical treatment centre. The west front with its pillared portico, originally sheltering a free pump for water-drinkers, is a simple but striking example of Wood's skill in utilising a confined space to the best effect.

Neither of these useful developments met the main problem, whose magnitude clearly daunted the Corporation. After timidly employing their Surveyor on minor works such as the provision of a pavilion to protect the King's Bath spring, a small pump-room for the Cross Bath and water-closets for the Pump Room itself, the Corporation finally appointed him Inspector of the Baths with the task of planning a complete overhaul of the bathing establishment. Baldwin's plan for this work was masterly and imposed for the first time an orderly design on the piecemeal untidiness of the area. In 1786 he had designed the colonnade to the north of the Pump Room and this formed the basis of his larger plan. He continued the colonnade on the southern side to accommodate the entrance to a set of new private baths and to the King's and Queen's Baths. Between the colonnades rose the new west front of the Pump Room. A hundred yards to the west lay the Cross Bath, in a dilapidated condition, and Wood's new Hot Bath. Between them and the Pump Room an ill-paved street of crumbling houses was the only link. Here Baldwin's genius took charge. He redesigned the Cross Bath, producing a lovely little building, with a curved frontage facing towards the Pump Room surmounted by a decorative chimney stack, with a pillared semi-circular portico on the north side. To provide access to the Pump Room he designed a street with a colonnaded pavement on both sides, opening out at either end into a fine segmented curve. Bathers could now make the journey under cover and in elegance. The Cross Bath was savaged by a later City Architect in the 1880s, but Bath Street, one of the small gems of urban architecture, remains much as Baldwin designed it. So at long last the baths were worthy of the city whose fortune they had

43 The Cross Bath (built by Thomas Baldwin, 1787)

44 The Bath Street Colonnade (built by Thomas Baldwin, 1791)

45 The Pump Room, and colonnade, from a
drawing by T. H. Shepherd, published 1829

made. Old John Wood himself would have been forced, however
grudgingly, to approve.

Baldwin's financial failure in 1793 meant that the new Pump
Room had to be completed by John Palmer, and it is not clear
how much of the finished design is Baldwin's. It may be that the
interior and the north front (with its Greek inscription *ΑΡΙΣΤΟΝ*

MEN Y'ΔΩP, meaning 'Water is best') are Palmer's. However this may be, the Pump Room, as one enters it from the eastern ante-room, strikes the true note of Georgian elegance. In this splendid room with its great columns, its curved recesses at each end, its musicians' gallery, one can still take the waters under the baleful eye of Beau Nash, whose statue by Prince Hoare stands in the eastern alcove. A fine long-case Tompion clock, especially made for the Pump Room, continues to mark the passage of time. Coffee has largely replaced the tea which was the favourite drink of the original patrons, but a small orchestra still plays in the alcove, and it is not difficult to people the scene with figures from the colourful heyday of England's finest spa.[1] Incidentally, the best-known portrait of Nash [frontispiece] hangs in the ante-room of the Pump Room. It was painted from life by William Hoare, the brother of Prince Hoare. There he stands with his brick-red face and his eternal white beaver, his bold and insolent stare showing obvious disapproval of the latter-day tourist.

Palmer, whose work on the Pump Room has just been mentioned, was Baldwin's most important contemporary. While Baldwin was occupied with the redesigning of the bathing establishment, Palmer was engaged on two major works of his own. Bath was now expanding northwards up the slopes of Lansdown, above the Royal Crescent, and it is in this area that his most notable achievements lie. High up on the hill, on a site even more dramatic than that of the Royal Crescent, he built his own curving terraces. Lansdown Crescent, with its flanking Places, sweeps across the hillside in three great strides, a masterful solution to an intensely difficult problem. The site is steep and uneven, but there is no hint of awkwardness in the position or design of the buildings. The landscape could have been designed for them, instead of the reverse. Lansdown Crescent lacks the superlative quality of the Royal Crescent: it is not *glorious*, but no comparison can lessen its beauty and elegance and the plain dignity of its tall frontages, which rise into the sky unhampered by neighbouring buildings. At its western end, on an even more precipitous slope, Somerset Place was built by Eveleigh, with all the charm and fantasy which characterise this unusual architect, and remains with its unusual and romantic broken pediment one

---

[1] In the late nineteenth century a concert-room was built onto the Pump Room on its eastern side to the design of Brydon, the architect of the Guildhall extensions, and his work here is reasonably sympathetic—except to the ear! Acoustically the room is a sad failure.

46 The Tompion clock made by Thomas
Tompion, 1709, in the Pump Room

47 The Pump Room today

48 Lansdown Crescent—a romantic view

49 (*opposite*) Lansdown Crescent (built by John Palmer, 1789–93)

of the most delightful creations of this period. Eveleigh himself deserves fuller treatment than he will get in this book. An artist of imagination and boldness, his independence and originality distinguish him from his contemporaries. Camden Crescent, on the eastern slope of the hill, is his work, while Grosvenor Place with its garlanded columns is all that was built of an ambitious and imaginative plan of his, which was to have included an hotel, houses and gardens leading down to the river.[1] It was the only scheme devised to integrate the Avon into the city, but collapsed through lack of money. No one since Eveleigh's day has used the river as a feature in the architectural planning of the city, and thus one of its main natural beauties has been almost entirely neglected. It is hard to think of any other city with architectural pretensions where the existence of a river has not been seized on and made a central feature.

But we must return to Palmer. At the same time as he was building Lansdown Crescent, he was engaged, lower down the

---

[1] Eveleigh's use of an uneven number of columns in the frontages of both these buildings still shocks the orthodox.

hill, on the other major work for which he will be remembered, St James's Square. Clearly inspired by Queen Square, it has been more fortunate than its predecessor in retaining much of its original form. Each side is designed as a single terrace, to give the palatial effect which had been Wood's main objective, and the opposite sides were originally identical; they still almost are. This is Bath's second and last great square. It has the good fortune not to be a main thoroughfare and it has a peace and dignity which Queen Square, with its ceaseless, angry traffic has to a large extent lost. The purist, however, may question the propriety of placing a square on a sloping site.

We are now nearing the end of the great period of Bath building. The Palladian day has gone and the Georgian age as a whole is drawing to a close. As the number of visitors increased, their quality, in terms of wealth and birth, diminished. The more popular the resort became, the less it was frequented by the fashionable world. This fact, together with the immense building programme already completed, meant that there was no longer, by the end of the century, a large unsatisfied appetite for fine lodgings and elegant public buildings. The speculators and those, like Eveleigh, who could not believe that the boom was over, went bankrupt or gave up.

What new building there was at the turn of the century was not in the old idiom. The inspiration of Rome, transmitted by Palladio and translated into English terms with such success, was now exhausted. Architects were turning to Greece as the true source of the classical style, and for a short while the simple lines and delicate ornament of Greek architecture replaced the heavier and more ornate Roman style which we know as Georgian. At the same time there was a growing rebellion against the classical style as a whole. The Gothic revival, destined to have a dominant effect on the whole of English architecture until the discovery of new building materials in modern times made its dogmas irrelevant, had begun. Already in 1797 Palmer had build Christ Church in Julian Road in the neo-Gothic style, and Saint Mary's, Bathwick, built by John Pinch in the second decade of the new century, is an outstandingly successful example of the same style. Like Palmer, Pinch was happy in either idiom, and he was

50 Somerset Place (built by John Eveleigh, c. 1790, and completed 1820)

51 Grosvenor Place
    (built by
      John Eveleigh, 1791)

engaged on Cavendish Crescent and Place, both in the traditional Georgian manner, at the same time as he was busy with Saint Mary's. His work in either manner lacks the brilliance of that of his best predecessors, and the virtue of sobriety has, with him, perhaps turned into dullness. Nevertheless, his Sion Hill Place, hidden among its trees on the north-western slopes of the city, has a peaceful dignity all its own. Completed in 1820 it is the last of the fine terraces, and if there is an air of sadness about it, it is perhaps because it represents the end of a great line.

For almost a hundred years Bath had been the scene of what would now be called an 'urban development' unique in England. Only in Edinburgh's New Town can anything comparable be seen. There, however, the Georgian area of the city has to compete with the Victorian Princes Street, and, a little further away, with the medieval city around the Royal Mile. Bath is simply Georgian. There is nothing to compete or blur the picture. Even the late Perpendicular Abbey is somehow assimilated and seems to belong to the century of those whose memorials cover its walls. There is a regrettable human tendency to attempt to add lustre to one thing or one place by identifying it with whatever is most famous of its kind. Bruges becomes the Venice of the North; Bath, not only for Landor, is the English Florence. Identifications of this sort are generally irrelevant and frequently ridiculous. Bath is not Florence any more than it is the second Rome which old John Wood dreamed of. Bath is itself, a great masterpiece of architecture, and like all great art, exists in its own right.

At the point in time which we have now reached, the city is, as a work of art, complete. As a stage for the acting out of the human comedy, however, it is still in use. We have still to watch the last scenes of the play, part farce, part melodrama, which began with the entrance of Beau Nash a century earlier.

VIII

$\mathcal{A}RTISTS$ $\mathcal{A}ND$ $ECCE\mathcal{N}TRICS$

The thirty years following Nash's death are the most brilliant in Bath's history. The techniques he had devised to enable nobility and commoners to mix easily with each other had succeeded to an extent which went beyond what he may have intended. Bath became popular. This process had begun before his death and was to continue until at last it ruined the city as a fashionable resort. But this was far ahead. The visitors' lists were still full of sonorous titles. In 1765, for example, they included three princes, four dukes, and a marquess, 24 earls (with their countesses), 14 viscounts and 12 barons. For reasons which might be interesting if they could be discovered there were four marchionesses to the single marquess, and 43 viscountesses—which seems excessive. An archbishop and five bishops represented the Lords Spiritual. Outnumbering the aristocratic visitors were the gentry, making more exacting and varied demands for entertainment. A peppering of uncouth but wealthy manufacturers and merchants made up the social mixture. Here then were the traditional patrons of the arts in a mood to spend money and a bobtail eager to imitate or outdo them. It was ordinary common sense for actors, musicians, portrait-painters and the rest to converge on Bath and make it their centre. Here too authors would find a rich mine of human material for satire and fiction.

It was in Bath during its golden age that some of the greatest figures of the literary and artistic scene made their first public reputations.

It has always been part of the duty of men of family, as potential ancestors, to make their contribution to the family portrait-gallery. The newly rich, lacking such evidence of distinction, at least opened the record by having themselves painted. A month at Bath provided the leisure required for the necessary sittings. The only problem was to find a painter whose appointment-book was not full for weeks to come. Incomparably the greatest painter to make his name at Bath was, of course, Gainsborough. The story of his arrival in Bath and his later departure for London concerns Philip Thicknesse, his sponsor, more perhaps than Gainsborough, and will be told later. It is sufficient to record that he arrived in 1759 from Ipswich at the age of 32 with a small local reputation, no money and a wife to support. His success was immediate. He was soon overwhelmed with commissions and was prosperous enough to take a house in the Circus in 1766. Houses were not numbered at this time and there is evidence that the commemorative plaque on No. 24 should really be on No. 17. When the noise and bustle of the Circus proved too much for him he moved to an unidentified house at the top of Lansdown Road, retaining his 'town house' for sittings. In 1774 he left Bath for London.

Gainsborough had the irritating habit of neither signing nor dating his works. It is therefore not possible to say with certainty in every case which of his paintings belong to his Bath period, and the city possesses none of them. It seems however probable that the famous 'Blue Boy' was painted in Bath. He painted portraits not only of notable visitors like Laurence Sterne, the author of *Tristram Shandy* and Lord Clare, Goldsmith's host at Bath, but of many of the resident celebrities who appear elsewhere in this book. Sarah Siddons, her fellow-actors Quin and Henderson, Christopher Anstey the poet, Elizabeth Linley and her family and the egregious Mrs Macaulay all sat to him. His portrait of Captain Wade, Master of Ceremonies, was commissioned to be hung in the new Assembly Rooms but has since been sold. From Bath Gainsborough regularly sent his work to London for exhibition and he was elected a founder-member of the Royal Academy in 1768. He appears to have enjoyed the life of Bath and in particular the theatre, where he was a keen admirer of

Henderson, then its leading actor. He was also passionately fond of music, for which he had a natural talent, and fine instruments had an irresistible appeal for him. One, belonging to Mrs Thicknesse, played a part in the quarrel which led to his leaving Bath.

The second painter whose brilliant career began in Bath was Thomas Lawrence. The son of a Devizes inn-keeper, Lawrence was a boy-prodigy. He came to Bath in 1780 at the age of 11, already highly skilled in the art of pastel portraiture, and was at once taken up by society. He worked with astonishing speed, taking little more than a day over a portrait. At 18 he left Bath for good to become a student at the Royal Academy schools. He was to become the most fashionable portrait-painter of the day and to be knighted as President of the Royal Academy.

Whereas for Gainsborough and Lawrence Bath was a stepping-stone to London and world fame, for William Hoare the procedure was reversed. Beginning his career as a painter in London, he moved to Bath on his marriage in about 1740 and remained there until his death over fifty years later. During this time he painted most of the Bath celebrities, some more than once. Like Gainsborough a founder-member of the Royal Academy, he is undoubtedly the outstanding painter truly belonging to Bath. A number of his best portraits have remained in the city. His famous portrait of Nash in the Pump Room has already been mentioned; there is another in the Guildhall, where there are also his portraits of Ralph Allen, Pitt, Anstey and John Palmer, the pioneer of the Bath theatre whose work will be described later in this chapter. His crayon portraits of Chesterfield and Pope are in the National Portrait Gallery. Hoare was a friend of Ralph Allen and a constant visitor at Prior Park. His life and work span the whole of Bath's heyday. Prince Hoare, whose statue of Nash is in the Pump Room, was William Hoare's brother, and William's son, also Prince Hoare, was both artist and dramatist.

More popular, and more prosperous, than any of the foregoing was Thomas Barker—'Barker of Bath'. A member of a family of artists, he came as a young man to Bath where his talents impressed Charles Spackman, a wealthy coach-builder and patron of the arts. Spackman paid for him to go to Rome for four years to study painting and on his return Barker set up in Bath.

Here, apart from painting portraits—his picture of himself with Spackman is in the Guildhall—he specialised in rural scenes. His landscapes and rural figures made an enormous appeal to a public whose tastes were becoming increasingly romantic and 'sentimental' in the eighteenth-century sense. Examples are to be seen in the Holburne of Menstrie Museum in the city. His most famous work, *The Woodman*, was his third version of a subject which, originally taken from a picture by Gainsborough, had preoccupied him on and off since boyhood. It became immensely popular and reproductions were to be found in almost every home. His work had an extraordinary vogue and versions in pottery and fabric widened its artistic and commercial appeal. He was able to build himself a fine house at Sion Hill overlooking the city, where he exhibited a dramatic thirty-foot long fresco of the Turkish attack on Scion. Barker's work belongs both in date and mood to the early years of the following century and has little connection with Bath except as the place in which it was carried out.

While the portrait-painters recorded the features of the eminent their entertainment was a matter for other artists, in particular the musicians and actors. Nash, it will be remembered, had brought the first small orchestra of six musicians to Bath and soon music was provided in all the main places of assembly, even at breakfast time in Spring Gardens. The Abbey naturally had its organist, and this position was filled for thirty years or more, until his death in 1766, by Thomas Chilcott, a musician of distinction. It was he who first taught music to Thomas Linley, who, with his gifted children, ruled over the musical life of the city for twenty years. Linley was a man of remarkable musical talent and administrative ability. For many years he was the director of music at the Assembly Rooms, where he both managed the concerts, engaging the best-known performers of the day, and was himself the regular conductor. He was an enthusiastic lover of the works of Handel which had been much neglected after the composer's death, and is credited with having restored them to their rightful place in popular esteem. Linley's children were among the leading performers at his concerts. Of his sons, Thomas was a violinist who had made a deep impression on

Mozart while studying in Italy; Samuel was a talented oboist. Unhappily both died young. Their sisters, Elizabeth and Mary, were both singers. Of the two, Elizabeth, the elder, was incomparably the more gifted. From early childhood she had possessed a voice of perfect pitch and great sweetness. Taught by her father, she gave her first public performance at the age of 12 and from then on was in constant demand. As she matured, her voice acquired a brilliance and emotional range which made her the unrivalled star of Linley's concerts. She excelled especially in the solo parts of Handel's oratorios. Even more than her talent it was her beauty and modest charm which captivated Bath. Everyone fell in love with her. In the records of the day there is a unanimity of admiration which is still astonishing. A girl who could charm Fanny Burney on the one hand and a cynical rake like John Wilkes on the other must have possessed universal attractions. No wonder that Horace Walpole in a letter in 1773 records that the King 'admires her and ogles her as much as he dares in so holy a place as an oratorio'. She was painted by Reynolds as Saint Cecilia, the patron saint of music, and several times by Gainsborough.

Inevitably Elizabeth Linley was beset by suitors, and it is sad and extraordinary that the one chosen by her father as her future husband was a wealthy man of 60 called Long. The announcement of the betrothal caused an uproar, in London as well as in Bath. The universal assumption, certainly well-founded, was that Linley's choice was prompted by the elderly wooer's riches. It was equally certain that his daughter's wishes had no place in the transaction. Society was shocked and stirred by sympathy for the girl who dutifully accepted her father's decision. Samuel Foote, the comedian and playwright, was in Bath at the time. It was his particular procedure as a dramatist to satirise living personalities on the stage of the theatre in the London Haymarket of which he was the lessee. The story of Elizabeth Linley was rich material for him. He quickly wrote 'The Maid of Bath' in which Miss Linnet, young and lovely, is betrothed to one Solomon Flint, 'an old, fusty . . ., water-drinking, milk-marring, amorous old hunks'. The play, in which everyone recognised the characters, was a considerable success, but arrangements for Elizabeth's wedding went inexorably on. It was only at the last moment, after the marriage-settlement had been agreed, that the wretched girl approached her elderly fiancé and begged to be released from her engagement. Long, to his credit, not only agreed but, to protect Elizabeth's good name, took the initiative in breaking the contract. Incredibly, Linley threatened to take him to court, whereupon Long, who was obviously a very different person from Foote's caricature, agreed to settle £3,000 on Elizabeth and allowed her to keep the jewels which were to have been his wedding present to her. Long's generosity is in telling contrast with Linley's sordid attempt to exploit his daughter's attractions. If as a father Linley was less than admirable he was still a first-rate musician and impresario. In 1775 he decided to leave Bath for London at the request of Sheridan, for whom he had composed the music for *The Duenna*. He was appointed Director of Music at Drury Lane and his later career was as successful as had been his career in Bath.

Meanwhile in 1761 a young Hanoverian musician named Herschel had appeared in Bath. An accomplished instrumentalist and a capable conductor and teacher, he soon acquired a reputation and was appointed organist at the newly opened Octagon Chapel, the most fashionable of the proprietary chapels. When Linley migrated to London, Herschel was the obvious choice as his successor, and for a number of years held the position of musical director at the Rooms. Herschel, however, had a second interest which at an early stage supplanted music as his main preoccupation; he was an amateur astronomer. With little spare time and less money, he devoted both to his hobby. Unable to afford a telescope, he made one of his own, the first in a series of ever more powerful instruments which his search of the heavens made necessary to him. Soon the house he shared with his sister Caroline, herself a professional singer of talent, became little more than a workshop in which he spent every moment he could spare. He still depended on music as his sole source of income and would hurry home late at night after a concert and, still in his lace and ruffles, settle down to work at his bench. He constantly went without sleep and would have gone without food if his sister had not fed him as he worked. The story of the construction of his great mirror has much the same dramatic quality as Benvenuto Cellini's account of the casting of his Orpheus, with additional comic overtones. The mirror was needed for a thirty-foot reflector and the material used for the mould was, improbably enough, powdered horse-dung in vast quantities. Not only the long-suffering Caroline but every visitor to the house was forced to take a turn at pounding this unattractive material until there was enough for the purpose. When finally the moment for casting arrived and the melted metal was ready to pour the container sprang a leak and molten metal shot all over the basement in which the oven stood. Herschel and his assistants managed to escape unharmed but the sudden heat exploded the stone floor. A second attempt was a complete success. So too were Herschel's observations. In 1781 he discovered a new planet, later to be named Uranus, and thus became the first astronomer to add to the number of known planets since the days of antiquity. In the following year his pre-eminence was recognised by his appointment as Astronomer Royal, and he left Bath for London.

The Rooms were once more without a musical director. In Herschel's place Venanzio Rauzzini, an Italian opera-singer, was appointed. It was a wise appointment and Rauzzini, until his death twenty years later, provided regular musical entertainment of high quality. It must be added that he was a better musician than businessman and the concerts showed a steady loss.

During Nash's reign the theatre in Bath had had an undistinguished history. The building was inadequate and performances no better attended than their poor quality deserved. After the suppression of public playhouses in 1736 the only theatrical entertainment in Bath was provided on makeshift stages, of which the least unsuitable was in the basement—John Wood called it a cellar—of Simpson's Rooms. Barbeau quotes the description of a French visitor in 1750 who was astonished 'to see your little theatre forty feet under the ground'. He thought it 'a pretty little catacomb' but 'somewhat stunted in its proportions'. He was not impressed by the standard of acting either. The performance of one of the leading actresses was marred by 'everything that the coarsest affectation could invent in the way of offensive grimaces to spoil a pretty face'. Clearly some action was called for, and in 1747 an actor named Hippisley launched a scheme for a new theatre, to be built by subscription, which would support a company of actors of better quality than had hitherto been maintained in Bath. He had the enthusiastic backing of John Wood, who made plans for a theatre of suitable size in Orchard Street, but died before work could start. In the following year John Palmer, a wealthy brewer, adopted the scheme, which attracted such support that building began without delay. The building was designed, not by Wood but probably by Thomas Jelly. In 1766 Palmer died and his son renovated the interior of the theatre, with so little success that the auditorium had to be entirely reconstructed in 1775 by Palmer's architect-namesake, the later designer of Lansdown Crescent. Meanwhile the theatre had achieved such a high reputation that Palmer succeeded in obtaining for it the grant of the title 'Royal', the first theatre outside London to be so honoured. The building is still standing but was badly damaged in the 1942 air-raids and is no longer in use. During its short life of little more than half a century, after which the much larger Theatre Royal in Beaufort Square replaced it, it saw a series of theatrical triumphs and became the most distinguished provincial theatre in England.

Palmer, a man of energy and imagination, at the same time as running a theatre was following in the footsteps of Ralph Allen as a Post Office reformer. It was he who, against entrenched opposition from officials and interested contractors, introduced mail-coaches, called Flying Machines, to replace the slow and unsafe post-horse. His work in this connection took him all over the country, and he used his travels as a means of recruiting theatrical talent where he found it. Meanwhile his interest in rapid communication was enhanced by the fact that he controlled a theatre in Bristol as well as in Bath and needed a speedy means of transport between the two places in order to use his actors in both theatres. The fast coaches with which he revolutionised the postal service were perhaps first developed for this purpose. Palmer later became Comptroller-General of the Post Office, where his career was brief, stormy but ultimately profitable to him. He became Mayor of Bath and for six years its M.P.

Under Palmer the theatre in Bath reached its highest dis-

THE *ORIGINAL* BATH MAIL COACH.
Invented by Mr Palmer of BATH, and Supported by GOVERNMENT.

52 Palmer's 'Flying Machine'

tinction. It was he who engaged John Henderson on Garrick's recommendation, and it was in Palmer's theatre that Henderson made the name which was to take him, after five years at Bath, to London as Garrick's natural successor and the leading English actor. Henderson had been much struck by a young actress whom he had seen performing in Birmingham, and recommended her to Palmer, who engaged her. As she had recently been dismissed by Garrick after a few unsuccessful months at Drury Lane, no doubt she was glad to have the chance to act once more before a fashionable audience. This time there was no failure; Sarah Siddons' début at Bath in 1778 was a triumph. She was an immediate and phenomenal success, particularly in tragic rôles. Her Lady Macbeth and Desdemona were magnificent, and she made a special reputation as Hamlet in Garrick's version of the play. Travelling constantly between Palmer's two theatres, and burdened by two young children (her husband, a dim figure, was not with her), she had an exhausting but sensational five years in Bath. In 1782 she returned in triumph to Drury Lane where Sheridan had taken over from Garrick. She stayed with Sheridan for seven years, and would doubtless have stayed longer if he had paid her salary more regularly. Her subsequent career was a series of triumphs. Her greatness is beyond question and the devotion she inspired first in Bath and then in London is probably unparalleled on the English stage. Even Dr Johnson, not much given to sentimental gestures, wrote his name on the hem of her dress in Reynold's portrait, so that, he said, he might thus share a little of her fame. As Davies rather clumsily expresses it in his *Dramatic Miscellanies*: 'the many accidents of spectators falling into fainting fits in the time of her acting bear testimony to the effects of her exertions'. With Henderson and Siddons, Bath's reputation as the nursery of the English stage was firmly established and was to endure into the next century, when, among others, Macready and Kean laid the foundation of their careers here; not, to be sure, in the Orchard Street theatre made famous by the great Sarah, but in Beaufort Square, where in 1805 a new Theatre Royal was built under the direction of John Palmer the architect.

The most famous theatrical name associated with Bath is, of

53 Sarah Siddons, by Thomas Gainsborough

course, Richard Brinsley Sheridan, although his career as a playwright and manager began only after he had left the city. Sheridan's father, Thomas, established himself in Bath in 1763 as a teacher of oratory (i.e. elocution). A former actor-manager in his native Dublin he is now known for little but his quarrel with Johnson, previously a close friend. In 1762 he received a state pension, and Johnson remarked, half-jocularly and half in earnest 'What, have they given *him* a pension? Then it is time for me to give up mine!' An acquaintance quickly carried the comment to Sheridan, who, in spite of Boswell's efforts as a peacemaker, never forgave Johnson.

Richard Sheridan, having finished his schooling at Harrow, joined his family in Bath in 1771. Here he at once fell in love, like everybody else, with Elizabeth Linley, at 17 the toast of the town. The story of his elopement with her, his duels on her behalf and their eventual marriage has been told many times, with Sheridan in the rôle of romantic hero. The main facts are fairly clear. Assisted by the charm which was to bewitch people all his life, Sheridan quickly took the lead over his rivals for Elizabeth's affection. Then in the spring of 1772 the pair vanished sensationally from Bath. Sheridan left behind a letter giving as the reason for their departure the urgent need to free Elizabeth from the dishonourable attentions of a Captain Mathews, a married man, and a friend both of himself and the Linley family. The pair were next heard of at Lille, where Elizabeth was housed in a convent, and whence, a month later, she was retrieved by her father. In the interval, Sheridan had declared his love and they had apparently been secretly married; whether this is so or not, certainly Elizabeth reciprocated her lover's feelings, without it seems, surrendering her virtue. Mathews meanwhile had published in the press a denial of Sheridan's accusations, labelled him a 'liar and treacherous scoundrel' and issued a general challenge to anyone spreading the slander originated by Sheridan. The latter returned to England immediately after Elizabeth and her father, located Mathews in London and fought a duel with him at the end of which Mathews begged for his life and gave Sheridan a written apology, which he at once published in the Bath Press. Bath society now shunned Mathews for what was regarded as cowardice and he left the city. After a few weeks he returned, demanding satisfaction from Sheridan, and a second duel was fought at Kingsdown on the outskirts of Bath. This was a bloody affair, more of a stabbing match than a duel in the accepted sense, which ended with both men on the ground hacking at each other with broken swords; Mathews emerged a clear winner, Sheridan receiving serious wounds from which he only recovered after some months. He then moved to London, where the Linleys now were, and in the following year married his Elizabeth.

It is an odd story, made odder by obvious inconsistencies inserted subsequently to enhance its romantic appeal. The version given in Sheridan's two main biographies relies totally upon an account written in old age by his sister Elizabeth Le Fanu—an inaccurate and romanticised narrative, in which her brother and Mathews appear respectively as penny novelette hero and double-dyed villain. As the events in question had occurred when she was a girl of 13 she may be forgiven for having forgotten the truth of the matter; her story is the contribution of a loyal sister to a favourite brother's reputation and it is a pity that this old lady's recollection should have been uncritically accepted in otherwise respectable literary works. There is in fact nothing but Sheridan's accusation to suggest that Mathews had dishonourable designs on Elizabeth and nothing but Elizabeth Le Fanu's statement to show that she felt obliged to run away with an attractive young man in order to escape them. In spite of Sheridan's assurances that his motives were completely disinterested, the fact remains that an elopement was an infallible means of compromising a lady in such a case, and a certain way of ensuring marriage if she were respectable. It would be in keeping with Sheridan's character if he had planned the flight as a shrewd move which he rightly forecast would win him the game. Nor do the duels with Mathews contribute anything to the picture of Sheridan as a romantic hero; they were nasty contests notable neither for swordsmanship nor fair play. In short, the episode appears to show the young Sheridan as already possessing the enormous charm and talent for getting his own way which enabled him, then and later, to get away with unscrupulous tactics which would have been condemned in a less attractive personality.

Sheridan's connection with Bath ends when his wounds are healed, and he leaves for London, marriage with Elizabeth and a brilliant future. Within a few years he had taken over control of Drury Lane from Garrick, was a highly successful playwright and was then to have an equally distinguished career in politics, to rival Burke as a Parliamentary orator and to be buried in Westminster Abbey. His life with Elizabeth, it is pleasant to record, was entirely happy.

Two of Sheridan's comedies are among the classics of the eighteenth-century theatre and they still sparkle brightly enough to be regularly performed. Both draw on his knowledge of Bath. *The School for Scandal* was originally entitled 'The Slanderers: A Pump Room Scene' and the action could well be laid in Bath. *The Rivals*, his first success, produced at Covent Garden within three years of his arrival in London, is actually set in Bath and gives a vivid picture of fashionable life in the city. The characters follow the daily round from Pump Room to gaming-table. As Fag, Captain Absolute's manservant says

In the morning we go to the Pump Room (though neither my master nor I drink the waters); after breakfast saunter on the Parades or play a game at billiards; at night we dance; but d—n the place, I'm tired of it; their regular hours stupefy me—not a fiddle nor a card after eleven.

The circulating libraries provide Lydia Languish with her reading —*Peregrine Pickle* and *The Innocent Adultery* for example—and with less heady literature for display on her dressing table— Fordyce's *Sermons* and Chesterfield's *Letters*. The framework of behaviour is provided by Nash's rules and the rivals themselves are careful to conceal under their coats the swords they need for their duel, since 'a sword seen in the streets of Bath would raise as great an alarm as a mad dog'. The back-cloth of the outdoor scenes is Wood's North Parade. The theme of the play is inescapably linked with Sheridan's own adventures, treated appropriately enough as pure comedy. Although Sheridan's contact with Bath had been brief, he had extracted the maximum dramatic material from his few years there. Ironic and

54 Mrs Richard Brinsley Sheridan (Elizabeth Linley), by Thomas Gainsborough

uncensorious, it is he more than anyone else who has painted Bath as it was in its fashionable heyday: gay, superficial, frivolous and spiteful, a suitable subject for irony indeed but not for any more solemn critical treatment.

Sheridan's is a valid attitude, but so too is Smollett's, two of whose novels, *Roderick Random* and *Humphrey Clinker*, are set partly in Bath. Smollett kept the season at Bath for a number of years, exercising his profession as a doctor, but he was never able to establish himself there in regular practice, in spite of having published a laudatory essay on the mineral waters. He therefore nourished a grudge against the city in keeping with his general bitterness against English society, which, he felt, rejected him because of his North British origin. *Humphrey Clinker* was probably first drafted when Smollett was living in Gay Street in 1766, but was published only after his death. The gouty, irascible but soft-hearted Matthew Bramble often speaks with the voice of the author, particularly as the satirist of Bath. He disapproved of the modish crowds and their daily routine:

Instead of that peace, tranquility, and ease, so necessary to those who labour under bad health, weak nerves, and irregular spirits; here we have nothing but noise, tumult, and hurry; with the fatigue and slavery of maintaining a ceremonial, more stiff, formal, and oppressive, than the etiquette of a German elector.

As for the architecture of the city, he grudgingly admits that Queen Square has merit:

The Square, though irregular, is, on the whole, pretty well laid out, spacious, open, and airy; and, in my opinion, by far the most wholesome and agreeable situation in Bath, especially the upper side of it; but the avenues to it are mean, dirty, dangerous and indirect.

Its main drawback, according to Bramble, is the absence of convenient access to the baths:

Communication with the Baths, is through the yard of an inn,[1] where the poor trembling valetudinarian is carried in a chair, betwixt the

---

[1] The White Hart. There was no satisfactory road linking the newly built Upper Town and the old city, where the baths lay, until Union Street was built in 1806.

heels of a double row of horses, wincing under the curry-combs of grooms and postillions, over and above the hazard of being obstructed, or overturned, by the carriages which are continually making their exit or entrance.

Bramble, doubtless expressing Smollett's own views, had nothing but contempt for the rest of the new building in Bath:

The rage of building has laid hold on such a number of adventurers, that one sees new houses starting up in every out-let and every corner of Bath; contrived without judgment, executed without solidity, and stuck together, with so little regard to plan and propriety that the different lines of the new rows and buildings interfere with, and inter- sect one another in every angle of conjunction. They look like the wreck of streets and squares disjointed by an earthquake.

The Circus in particular aroused his scorn. 'A pretty bauble, designed for shew', it looked to him 'like Vespasian's amphi- theatre turned inside out'. After criticising the shape of the rooms dictated by the curve of each segment of the Circus, he proposes that the wide areas in front of the houses should be covered in by an arcade, which would not only enhance their appearance, but provide protection from the rain, 'which is almost perpetual':

At present, [he says] the chairs stand soaking in the open street, from morning to night, till they become so many boxes of wet leather. . . . Indeed this is an inconvenience that extends over the whole city. . . . Even the close chairs, contrived for the sick, by standing in the open air, have their frieze linings impregnated, like so many spunges, with the moisture of the atmosphere, and these cases of cold vapour must give a charming check to the perspiration of a patient, piping hot from the Bath, with all his pores wide open.

The Circus was even more difficult of access than Queen Square. It was remote

from all the markets, baths and places of entertainment. The only entrance to it, through Gay Street, is so difficult, steep, and slippery, that, in wet weather, it must be exceedingly dangerous, both for those that ride in carriages, and those that walk a-foot.

Confusing John Wood the Elder with his son, he is sarcastic about the architectural destiny of the city:

The same artist, who planned the Circus, has likewise projected a Crescent; when that is finished, we shall probably have a Star, and those who are living thirty years hence, may, perhaps, see all the signs of the Zodiac exhibited in architecture at Bath.

The worst feature of the new buildings was, in Bramble's view, the material of which they were made. Ralph Allen's stone was soft and crumbling; his manservant Roger Williams 'or any man of equal strength, would be able to push his foot through the strongest part of their walls, without any great exertion of their muscles'. Smollett's scorn for the buildings of Bath is less a serious criticism than an expression of his general misanthropy. He concentrates his greatest venom on the inhabitants. His description of the fashionable company of Bath 'where a very inconsiderable proportion of genteel people are lost in a mob of impudent plebeians' is worth quoting for the bitterness of its invective:

Clerks and factors from the East Indies, loaded with the spoil of plundered provinces; planters, negro drivers, and hucksters, from our American plantations, enriched they know not how; agents, commissaries, and contractors, who have fattened, in two successive wars, on the blood of the nation; usurers, brokers, and jobbers of every kind; men of low birth, and no breeding, have found themselves suddenly translated into a state of affluence, unknown to former ages; and no wonder that their brains should be intoxicated with pride, vanity, and presumption. Knowing no other criterion of greatness, but the ostentation of wealth, they discharge their affluence without taste or conduct, through every channel of the most absurd extravagance; and all of them hurry to Bath, because here, without any further qualification, they can mingle with the princes and nobles of the land. Even the wives and daughters of low tradesmen, who, like shovel-nosed sharks, prey on the blubber of those uncouth whales of fortune, are infected with the same rage of displaying their importance; and the slightest indisposition serves them for a pretext to insist upon being conveyed to Bath, where they may hobble country dances and cotillons among lordlings, 'squires, counsellors and clergy.

Steele, commenting at an earlier stage on Nash's discovery of the secret of mixing the vulgar and the great, had said in the *Guardian* 'It was no little satisfaction to me to view the mixed masses of all ages and dignities upon a level, partaking of the same benefits of nature and mingling in the same diversions.' Steele and Smollett were describing different phases in a single process, and their descriptions are more than reflections of their own temperament. Nash had in fact been too successful in his campaign against snobbery; the vulgar had begun to take over.

Winifred Jenkins, Tabitha's maid in *Humphrey Clinker*, was for her part delighted with 'the fine shows of Bath' and excited by her experience of bathing 'with ne'er a smock on our backs, hussy'. Nor was Bramble's niece Lydia in the least displeased either by the life or the buildings of Bath. She was impressed by the Master of Ceremonies, Samuel Derrick, of whom more later, when he paid his courtesy call. The architecture entranced her; Bath seemed 'an earthly paradise' with the new buildings 'like so many enchanted castles, raised on hanging terraces'. Among the less naïve visitors, however, there was a growing consciousness both of the vacuity of the Bath routine and of the absurdity of the airs and affectations of the uncultivated visitors who jostled the gentry in the Rooms and on the Parades. It was better on the whole to laugh about it all than to waste energy on indignation.

A satirist whose purpose reflected the tolerant amusement felt by many visitors published his single masterpiece in 1766, while Smollett was living in Bath and writing his splenetic novel. Christopher Anstey's *New Bath Guide* is a light-hearted verse-satire on life in Bath which still gives pleasure. It is written as a series of letters, mostly in a skipping anapaestic metre which was to set a fashion in light verse. The adventures of Simkin Blunderhead, his sister Jenny and their maid Tabitha among the doctors, Methodists and fortune-hunters of Bath delighted Anstey's readers and the book was sensationally successful; so much so that the publisher Dodsley, after ten editions, restored to the author the copyright he had originally bought from him, saying that no other book had paid so well and so fast. Even Horace Walpole, usually as sour a critic as Smollett, was enthusiastic in its praise. Writing to a friend, he said:

What pleasure you have to come! There is a new thing published that will make you bepiss [sic] your cheeks with laughing. It is called the New Bath Guide. . . . So much wit, so much humour, fun and poetry, so much originality, never met together before.

Simkin Blunderhead has come to Bath to take the cure. On arriving at his lodgings he is serenaded by the town band in the usual way:

> *If a broker or stateman, a gamester or peer,*
> *A nat'ralis'd Jew, or a bishop comes here;*
> *Or an eminent trader in cheese should retire,*
> *. . . . . . .*
> *With horns and with trumpets, with fiddles and drums,*
> *They'll strive to divert him as soon as he comes.*

Simkin's doctors prescribe a course of the waters, of which none of them has personal experience:

> *Since the Day that King Bladud first found out thê bogs,*
> *And thought them so good for himself and his hogs,*
> *Not one of the Faculty ever has try'd*
> *These excellent'waters to cure his own hide.*

Tabitha also takes the waters. Simkin catches her just before she sets out:

> *I went up and found her*
> *In a blanket, with two lusty fellows around her,*
> *Who both seem'd a-going to carry her off in*
> *A little black box just the size of a coffin.*

At the baths Simkin finds the spectacle enchanting:

> *Twas a glorious sight to behold the fair sex*
> *All wading with gentlemen up to their necks,*
> *And view them so prettily stumble and sprawl*
> *In a great smoking kettle as big as our hall.*

While Simkin is enjoying the familiar round of public breakfasts, balls and card-playing, Jenny is being pursued by Captain Cormorant, a fortune-hunting gamester who had already cheated Simkin at lansquenet. Tabitha, for her part, is soon in the toils of a rascally Moravian preacher whose religious philosophy is based on the view that

> *There is neither transgression nor sin,*
> *A doctrine that brings many customers in.*

Most aspects of the life and society of Bath are touched on in the poem, with a gaiety and charm that made its satirical content doubly palatable to its readers. One who not only read the poem but turned it to his own use was Smollett, who used it shamelessly as a source, both of episodes and characters, for *Humphrey Clinker*. The well-known passage in which Matthew Bramble is roused to fury, first by the 'strange kind of thumping and bouncing' caused by Sir Ulic Mackilligut's dancing lessons in the rooms above his own, and then by the din of French horns being played ten feet from his door by the negro servants of a Creole lodger, is drawn directly from Anstey's account of Lord Ringbone in agonies of gout brought on by the noise of music and dancing overhead. Tabitha's infatuation with her Moravian parson is reflected in the emotions felt by Winifred Jenkins for the Methodist Humphrey Clinker. Aunt Tabitha Bramble's romantic attachment for Mackilligut and Cormorant's pursuit of Jenny are unmistakably similar. Anstey's Cormorant, too, is blood-brother to Smollett's Lieutenant Lismahago. There are other strong resemblances between the two works which, together with Smollett's established practice of using living characters and events for his own fictional purposes, make clear that borrowing—or theft—has occurred, and who was the borrower.

Anstey, a wealthy country squire, was Member of Parliament for Trumpington, a village and pocket borough just outside Cambridge, and his poem takes its metre and style from satirical works currently in vogue at both universities. Shortly after the appearance of the *New Bath Guide* he moved to Bath, where he lived in a house in the Royal Crescent and enjoyed his fame as a poet, a fame which rests on one poem, for although he wrote other verse, none of it has the least merit. A man of great charm, he was popular in Bath society. He received an especially warm welcome, as one of their own craft, from the Water Poets of Batheaston, who must now be given the notice which is their due.

Among Walpole's hosts when he stayed at Bath in the year Anstey's poem appeared were a Captain and Mrs Miller, who entertained extensively at their villa at Batheaston, a village two miles away from the city. The Captain is a shadowy figure, but his wife has earned one of those special places in social history reserved for the memorably fatuous. Lady Miller, as she later became, had literary as well as social pretensions. In 1775, after

55 The Batheaston vase

returning from a cultural trip to Italy, she inaugurated weekly poetical contests at her house. Here an aristocratic assembly of guests, selected on grounds of respectability as much as birth, competed in writing sets of verses on themes announced by the hostess or in composing *bouts rimés*. In the latter form of contest, a poem of half a dozen lines had to be fitted to a set of rhymes, often in the form of an 'enigma', that is, a riddling description of an object. The verses were deposited in a vase brought back from Frascati by the Millers, and held, as a matter of faith rather than fact, to have been the property of Cicero. They were then drawn out and declaimed, and the authors of the three poems voted the best were crowned with wreaths of myrtle by the 'Institutress'. The Batheaston *soirées* had an enormous vogue; it was not exceptional to see fifty carriages at the door, and the highest recorded score of duchesses was four. When a selection of the verses was published in 1776, the edition was sold out in ten days and three more volumes appeared in quick succession. The poems have no merit of any kind, except perhaps as evidence of what might be called the absurdity-potential of the human race. Lady Miller's own contributions are easily the most stupid and the clumsiest. The silly côterie which produced this nonsense richly deserves the ridicule poured on it, without noticeable effect, by Johnson and Walpole. Steele, as we have seen, had invented the title of the Water Poets to describe the witless rhymesters who infested Bath in the early years of the century and it is appropriate that Lady Miller's guests should have assumed the title with due pride.

Among Lady Miller's contemporaries, two more ladies, equally ambitious, almost as silly, more able than she but less amiable, deserve attention. Selina, Countess of Huntingdon, took religion as her field, and made it her own. An early convert to the teachings of Wesley, she appears to have held her enthusiasm for the new doctrines under reasonable control until the death of her husband in 1747. From then on however she devoted all her immense energy and considerable wealth to the sect, of which, as the most notable adherent of noble birth, she coolly assumed she ought to have the leadership. She was, in fact, admitted to the small council which directed its affairs, where she made life difficult for her socially inferior colleagues. She set about building chapels all over the country, trained and appointed ministers for them, and ruled in detail over the lives and religious opinions of her followers; she made it abundantly clear that the chapels of 'The Countess of Huntingdon's Connexion' and the ministers who served them were 'hers' in every sense, and tolerated not the slightest indiscipline or deviation from the doctrine which she laid down for their observance.

In 1765 she built a chapel in Bath, where she had already spent much of her time, busy about the conversion of the world of fashion. Large and distinguished audiences collected, under pressure from her, to hear the preaching of Wesley and Whitefield and some were converted to their teachings. An unlikely supporter, though not technically a convert, was Chesterfield,

56 Selina, Countess of Huntingdon (artist unknown)

now over 70. Not so Nash, who had a series of skirmishes with the reformers who threatened his way of life. Wesley, having opened his religious campaign in London in 1738, had come in the following year to Bath, where to his astonishment 5000 attended his first two sermons. 'Can the Gospel have a place where Satan's throne is?' he asked. Satan in the person of the King of Bath made an attempt at one of these meetings to talk down the preacher. It was a sad failure. Now that a lady of rank headed the movement in Bath, Nash felt it incumbent on himself to give it some slight personal recognition. He therefore accepted an invitation to hear Whitefield speak in Lady Huntingdon's house in Edgar Buildings—the chapel was not built in his lifetime— where he had to endure, not only the preacher's pointed references to his deplorable way of life, but subsequent ridicule when his visit became the talk of the town. He was particularly irritated by a broadsheet which was circulated to announce his conversion and forthcoming appearance as a preacher. Lady Huntingdon's manner with 'her' ministers was domineering and proprietorial, while theirs to her was servile and fawning, Whitefield's no less than that of her own appointees. Cardinal Newman was to refer to her later as 'Selina episcopa', but this title does less than justice to a woman who had to be Pope or nothing. Wesley grew tired of her ways; she always spoke, he said, of '*my* college, *my* masters, *my* students: "I" mixes with everything'. In 1770 she broke with him on doctrinal grounds and continued her Calvinistic way with Whitefield. After her death the 'Connexion' withered quickly away, and her chapels are now generally used by the Congregational or Presbyterian Churches.

Her chapel in the Vineyards at Bath is still in regular use as a Presbyterian chapel, its internal layout remaining much as it was when Walpole described it:

At the upper end is a broad 'hautpas' of four steps, advancing in the middle: at each end of the broadest part are two of my eagles with red cushions for the parson and clerk. Behind them rise three more steps, in the midst of which is a third eagle for pulpit. Scarlet armchairs for all three. On either hand, a balcony for elect ladies.

As a building, the chapel is not remarkable, but the neo-Gothic manse in the courtyard screening it from the road is charming.

The third of the extraordinary women who demands attention was a historian of better education than the other two, and perhaps more absurd than either. Catherine Macaulay came to Bath as a widow in 1774. The author of a *History of England* she was already notorious as a 'leveller' or 'republican', that is, a believer in the equality of man. This doctrine, which she propagated unceasingly in her writings and conversation, was held scandalous in an age which regarded the differentiation of rank and station as a divinely ordained part of the social order. As a leveller she had been the victim of one of Johnson's best-known tricks. He pretended on one occasion to have been converted to her views, and on the strength of this proposed to invite her footman to sit at table with them when they were dining together. She never spoke to him again, affronted by the unfair suggestion that she should put her doctrines into practice. By the time she came to Bath she was already sufficiently notorious for her extreme political views; but there was more to come. She took up residence at No. 2 Alfred Street, owned and lived in by a Dr Wilson, the absentee rector of a London parish. He succumbed quickly to her charms and became in short order a besotted admirer, determined to go to all lengths to show his ardour. The height of enthusiasm and folly was reached in 1777, when he erected in St Stephen's, Walbrook, his London church, a statue in her honour, showing the lady as the Muse of History. Even this scandalous procedure did not, it seems, satisfy his passion for absurdity. In the same year he decided that her birthday should be appropriately celebrated. He arranged an evening party, at which six odes were solemnly declaimed in her honour, and the good parson presented her with a gold medal. Helping him on this great occasion was a Dr Graham—the 'advertising doctor' Thicknesse called him—a Scottish quack not yet at the peak of his notoriety. This was to be reached when he established in London in 1778 a Temple of Aesculapius whose main attraction was a 'Celestial Bed' which would, he claimed, 'electrify' the ladies and gentlemen who spent a night in it. Flimsily clad young ladies, in the role of 'Vestina, the Rosy Goddess of Health', welcomed potential customers. (One of them was a girl calling herself Emma Hart, then in her early teens, who later became the wife of the complaisant Sir William Hamilton, and Nelson's plump mistress.) Emboldened by a certain success, Graham moved his bed to Pall Mall, where he opened what he now frankly called the Temple of Hymen, devoted to the 'great business of conception'.

The improved Celestial Bed, he announced in his advertisement, 'rests on six massy and transparent columns; coverings of purple, and curtains of celestial blue surround it, and the bedclothes are perfumed with the most costly essences of Arabia'. Its efficacy, if that is the right word, depended on a number of magnets

so disposed and arranged, as to be continually pouring forth in an ever-flowing circle, inconceivable [this is surely the wrong word!] and irresistibly powerful tides of the magnetic effluvium, which every philosophical gentleman knows has a very strong affinity with the electrical fire. These magnets, too, being pressed, give that charming springyness—that sweet undulating, tittulating, vibratory, soul-dissolving, marrow-melting motion; which on certain critical and important occasions, is at once so necessary and so pleasing.

The fee was now doubled, but the genteel public was apparently loth to admit its need of Graham's aid and the venture failed.

At the time of Mrs Macaulay's birthday party, these events lay a few years ahead; at this stage Graham was merely one of the leading quacks of Bath. Graham and Catherine Macaulay had a lively admiration for each other; at the birthday party he presented her with a copy of his *Works*, in which he claimed 'under God' (a nice tribute) the credit for curing her of 'the complicated and obstinate maladies your fair and delicate frame was afflicted with'. She for her part recorded, in a letter reproduced in the *Works*, her support for his claim. 'A great part,' she says, 'of my disease immediately gave way to your Balsamic Essences, and to your Aerial, Aetherial, Magnetic and Electrical Appliances and Influences.' With such distinguished support Dr Wilson's party could not fail to be a resounding success, and he was entitled to believe that a tribute of this kind would give him a unique place in the esteem and—who could tell?—the heart of the recipient.

It is sad to record that he was mistaken. A year later she married the 21-year-old brother of Dr Graham, whose cure of her 'disease' was not perhaps as complete as it might have been. The ineffable Wilson flew into an un-Christian rage, dismantled the monument he had put up and sold the vault he had purchased as the resting-place for her remains.

One of the less reliable sources of information about Mrs Macaulay as well as other Bath personalities and events is to be found in the writings of Philip Thicknesse to which reference has already several times been made. Thicknesse himself qualifies for a high place in the roll of eccentrics associated with Bath. 'He had,' said Fulcher, the biographer of Gainsborough, 'in a remarkable degree the faculty of lessening the number of his friends and increasing the number of his enemies. He was perpetually imagining insult and would sniff an injury from afar.' The statement is true as far as it goes, but does less than justice to a man who, gifted with enough charm to acquire friends with some ease, seized the earliest opportunity of picking a quarrel with each of them in turn, and then pursued it with unparalleled violence and persistence, using every weapon available in an age when there was no effective law of libel.

Philip Thicknesse was a penniless Captain of Marines on half-pay when he arrived in Bath with his wife and three children around about 1750. The story of his marriage a few years earlier is typical of the man. His future bride was widely rumoured to inherit a fortune on the death of her father. Desperately seeking a wealthy match but distrusting rumour, Thicknesse made a special trip to London to inspect the relevant will. Satisfied with what he found, he opened his campaign. He was soon victorious with the lady but failed to recommend himself to her family. He therefore resorted to an elopement, always a reliable basis for a family quarrel. Unhappily for his expectations, his wife and two of his children died in a diphtheria epidemic in Bath, and he himself almost followed them. Philip Gosse, his biographer, quotes the letter in which he informed his wife's mother of these events:

Madam, your daughter is dead, your grand-children are dead, and I apprehend I am dying: but if I recover, the greatest consolation I have is, that now I have no more to do with you.

Thicknesse's second marriage to Lady Elizabeth Touchet,

daughter of the Earl of Castlehaven, in 1754 was more fortunate. She brought him a dowry which enabled him to purchase the governorship of Landguard Fort, the fortress guarding Harwich harbour. She also presented him with six children before dying following childbirth, after nine years of marriage. With the two sons of the marriage, the elder of whom inherited the Barony of Audley, Thicknesse was later to carry on a bitter feud. While at Landguard, he contrived, on the most trivial grounds, to quarrel with a Colonel Vernon, who commanded the regiment supplying the garrison for the fort. He conducted the quarrel like a military operation, with letters to the Secretary of State, the issue of a libellous broadsheet distributed free in large numbers in Ipswich, where Vernon was then standing for Parliament, and finally with a gross public insult in the shape of a wooden gun exhibited in the High Street of the town as a symbol of Vernon's military capacity. Predictably, Vernon took him to court and Thicknesse was sentenced to a fine and three months' imprisonment.

An extraordinary aspect of this and other equally humiliating and revealing episodes is that they were all published in well-documented detail by Thicknesse himself in his three volumes of Memoirs and Anecdotes which appeared from 1788 to 1791.

Within six months of the death of his second wife Thicknesse married her friend Ann Ford, who had been staying with Elizabeth during her last confinement and had stayed on to look after the children. The third and last Mrs Thicknesse was a beauty (as is shown by Gainsborough's portrait of her now in the Cincinatti Art Museum), a singer, a performer on the *viol da gamba* and the musical glasses and a favourite of London and Bath society. Not content with giving private concerts, she longed for the fame of public performances. Her father however was fiercely opposed to the exhibition of his daughter's talents and person in this way and imprisoned her at his London house to prevent it. She managed to escape and to make arrangements for a subscription concert at a theatre in the Haymarket, only to find that her parent had blockaded the theatre with constables from Bow Street. It was only when a friend in the Guards threatened to bring in his troops that the police dispersed and Ann at last gave her concert, which was a resounding success.

A woman of determination as well as gifts, perhaps she was the best kind of wife for Thicknesse. At all events their marriage seems to have been a happy one, and as his widow she wrote an epitaph in which appears the remarkable statement that 'no man ever was his enemy whose friendship was worth coveting'.

During his time as Governor of Landguard Fort, Thicknesse made the acquaintance of Thomas Gainsborough, then a struggling young painter at Ipswich. Thicknesse claims to have recognised his genius at once and to have been the first to do so. It is certainly true that he persuaded him to seek his fortune in Bath, where Thicknesse had a house and spent the winter months. The friendship followed the normal course. After a warm beginning in which Thicknesse undoubtedly exerted himself nobly on behalf of his protégé, the inevitable quarrel broke out. Gainsborough failed to complete a portrait of Thicknesse to go with the one he had painted of his wife. Thicknesse was incensed by what he regarded as base ingratitude and pursued the painter, one of the most peaceable and inoffensive of men, with violently expressed reproaches in the Assembly Rooms and by letter. When Ann Thicknesse joined in the attack, Gainsborough, according to Thicknesse, fled at once from Bath to London. Here Thicknesse, if he is to be believed, continued his patronage—the only occasion on which he is recorded as burying the hatchet—and introduced him to potential clients among the nobility.

By this time Thicknesse had given up his military governorship and settled in Bath, gaining some sort of income at the E–O tables and by other less reputable means. Letting his house in the Crescent, he bought a cottage behind what is now Lansdown Place West. He employed the architect Eveleigh to restore and extend the cottage, which he called St Catherine's Hermitage, and embellished the grounds with romantic features of all kinds. Uncovering two or three Roman and 'early British' coffins during the course of these works, he removed the skeleton from one of the latter—identifying it as that of 'a beautiful Saxon virgin'—and used the stone coffin as a basin to receive the water from a stream in the grounds. The coffin of a Roman knight—so classified by Thicknesse—he emptied of its embalmed corpse and set aside for use at his own burial. Near the cottage he dug a cave into the hillside, decorated the entrance with a rough stone arch, and later erected there the first memorial to Thomas Chatterton, the boy-poet and forger of the Rowley poems, who had recently committed suicide. In typically intemperate language Thicknesse described him as 'the Greatest Genius Britain, or perhaps any other nation under the sun, has produced'.

Among Thicknesse's numerous feuds in Bath was one with Samuel Foote, the actor and playwright. Foote had written a comedy, *A Trip to Calais,* in which the character of Kitty Crocodile was a satirical and easily recognisable portrait of the notorious Duchess of Kingston, whose marriage to the duke had recently been declared bigamous. The 'Duchess' objected violently in a series of fierce letters of which Thicknesse was widely and with reason thought to have been the author. Foote was, needless to say, until this time a friend of Thicknesse. He was finally forced to withdraw the play, and rewrote it omitting the cause of offence. He took his revenge on Thicknesse, however, by introducing him into the play under the name of Dr Viper, a name which his enemies delighted to use thereafter. Foote was as talented in the use of invective as Thicknesse, whom he described as having 'the stupidity of an owl, the vulgarity of a blackguard, the obdurate heart of an assassin and the cowardice of a dunghill cock'.

Under the will of their grandfather, the Earl of Castlehaven, Thicknesse's two sons inherited fortunes and the elder was also heir to the Barony of Audley, to which he became entitled during his father's lifetime, while still a young man. For Thicknesse, whose whole life was devoted to an unsuccessful effort to acquire wealth, the thought that his sons were already rich without any effort on their part was enough to infuriate him beyond measure and to antagonise him permanently against them. Following his usual policy towards those he chose as enemies, he began to attack his sons' characters, accusing the elder not only of filial neglect but of the responsibility for the death of a girl he had seduced. He branded Philip the younger son as a cheat. When Thicknesse was off on one of his many foreign trips, Philip had bought St Catherine's Hermitage from his father. He spent a good deal of money on it and on his father's return offered it back to him for less than he had paid in the first place. Thicknesse's reaction to what was a generous offer was to deny that Philip had in fact paid him at all, and produced what he claimed was documentary evidence to this effect. There was of course no substance in his allegation. No wonder that the sons took their mother's name of Touchet as soon as they were old enough to make the choice. Thicknesse gives his own version of his relationship with his sons, together with a scathing denunciation of their characters, in his Memoirs; the violence of his accusations and the intemperance of his language do not, however, obscure the total lack of evidence for his allegations. Even the title-page of the Memoirs is used by their author to publicise the quarrel; in it Thicknesse describes himself as

LATE
Lieutenant Governor
OF
LANDGUARD FORT
AND UNFORTUNATELY
father to GEORGE Touchet
BARON AUDLEY

Not content with blackening his sons' characters while he lived, he pursued the elder from beyond the tomb. His will included the following charming bequest:

I leave my right hand, to be cut off after death, to my son, Lord Audley, and I desire it may be sent to him in hopes such a sight may remind him of his duty to God, after having so long abandoned the duty he owed his Father who once affectionately loved him.

If many of Thicknesse's actions have a lunatic quality, it is possible that a long addiction to opium may be partly to blame. He suffered all his life from gallstones and regularly took heroic doses of laudanum to deaden the pain. By this means and by riding a trotting horse he claimed to have cured himself, voiding no less than twenty-seven stones in one day and applauding himself as 'the first and best gall doctor in England'.

Whether or not Thicknesse qualified in detail for Foote's unfriendly characterisation quoted above, it seems certain that he was, if not an assassin, at least a blackmailer. In his Memoirs he makes no secret of his technique in this field. At any time, he says, he could 'muster ten or a dozen knaves or fools who will put a hundred pounds or two into my pocket merely for holding them up to public scorn'. He printed privately a number of letters by Lady Mary Wortley Montague and obtained a useful sum of money from Lord Bute in return for an undertaking not to publish. It was an established practice of his to make gifts—sometimes of considerable value—to men of wealth or distinction and then demand favours from them in return. When they refused, as they often did, he threatened to expose their ingratitude to the public. The technique was not always successful, but Thicknesse was as happy to publish a scurrilous libel as to be paid to suppress it.

His only respectable source of income was from writing. He travelled a great deal on the continent and wrote accounts of his journeys which had a certain success. One of his books, not about his travels but about Bath, concerns us here and is still eminently readable. Stimulated by the success of Anstey's *New Bath Guide*, Thicknesse published in 1778 the *New Prose Bath Guide*. It purports to be a description of the city for the benefit of visitors, and in fact includes a good deal of information likely to be of use to them, though already available in the official publications of the spa authorities. What is of more interest is what the author has to say of the people and places he describes and the anecdotes with which he enlivens his account.

His scathing criticism of the arrangements for bathers at the King's Bath has already been quoted (page 62). He seems however to approve of Wood's newly built Hot Bath, which he ineptly describes as 'une petite Maison carée' [sic]. For the quality the Duke of Kingston's bath remains the only one where they can 'bathe decently'. He informs Lord North, to whom the book is dedicated, that 'we are BUILDING-MAD at BATH, my Lord, as well as in London', but has nothing but praise for the lodgings. 'It is in BATH alone, where People of Fashion can step out of their Coaches, after a long Journey, into Houses or Lodgings, full as warm and as comfortable as their own.'

He gives Nash full credit for having been the 'real founder of

Bath', and tells one or two stories about him;. but he cannot believe that Ralph Allen was as noble a person as he was generally held to be, and has characteristic sneers about his motives and even his well-known modesty of dress. He ridicules Catherine Macaulay and Dr Graham, whose claim for inclusion in a guide to Bath is obscure. He tells an amusing tale about the turnspit-dogs, then essential members of the kitchen staff in most good households. He tells how he was cured of gallstones. He warns bathers of the dangers of eating 'the spungy Part of hot Rolls, heightened by *burnt butter*'. In fact, it is a hotch-potch of a book, and failed to make a fortune for its author, though it is full of interest to the modern reader.

If the eighteenth century was an age of order, in which the chaos of the Middle Ages in both the physical and social spheres was swept away and replaced by new standards of propriety and formality, it was not yet bound by the conventions which it introduced. The foolish and eccentric were tolerated if not encouraged. Lady Miller could thrive on the witlessness of her *soirées*, and Dr Graham's Celestial Bed, though it was not a commercial success, attracted as much interest as ridicule. The extreme arrogance of the Countess of Huntingdon and the grotesque violence of Philip Thicknesse were resented only by those who were the direct sufferers. It would be wrong to suggest that the characters described in this chapter were truly representative of their time. But no account of eighteenth-century life would be complete if it ignored them. They throw their own light on an age whose social modes, sophisticated as they may appear, were in fact deeply different from any which have followed.

IX

DECLINE

As we have seen, the period immediately following Nash's death
was the time of Bath's greatest splendour, both architecturally
and as a centre of the arts. Socially, however, signs of decay were
already present.

Nash's campaign to break down the rigid barriers of rank and
degree and force the different social classes to mix, whether they
liked it or not, was a success only as long as he was alive to see
that they did so. Only an autocrat as powerful as Nash could
make the duchesses and drapers' wives be nice to each other.
When he died no one could be found to succeed him as an effective social dictator. Later Masters of Ceremonies were nonentities
with none of his authority; there was no King of Bath after Nash.
The fragile structure which he had built was not strong enough
to withstand the pressure of the snobs and vulgarians. Inevitably the more numerous the visitors who came to Bath, the
smaller the proportion of the well bred among them. Perhaps
even Nash could not have continued for long to preserve his
strict code of propriety and decorum. Certainly his successors
failed to do so.

Samuel Derrick, who became Master of Ceremonies in 1763,
after the brief incumbency of a French dandy called Collette,
was a fifth-rate poet, known to posterity largely through his
acquaintance with Dr Johnson, who 'had a kindness for him'. A
penniless Irishman, he had migrated to London where, after a
period as a linen-draper's assistant, he scraped a living on the

fringes of the literary world. According to Johnson, he 'would have been sweeping the crossings in the streets' if he had not been a writer. On hearing of his appointment as Master of Ceremonies at Bath, Johnson commented, 'Derrick may do very well, as long as he can outrun his character; but the moment his character gets up with him, it is all over'. He has acquired a kind of immortality as the victim of one of the doctor's typically offensive witticisms. Asked whether he reckoned Derrick or Smart the better poet, Johnson replied, 'Sir, there is no settling the point of precedency between a louse and a flea.' So much, apparently, for his literary talent; as for his other proclivities, it is suggestive that it was he who introduced Boswell to the life of London 'in all its variety of departments, both literary and sportive'. At all events, neither literature nor his gifts as a guide to the 'sportive' life of the metropolis provided him with an income big enough to give him a roof over his head, and he frequently slept in the streets. This was the man chosen to fill Nash's place. It was an absurd choice. In return for the £50 a year allowed him by the Assembly Rooms, the first and only regular income he ever had, he wrote insipid poems in honour of the more distinguished visitors, and was no more a Master of Ceremonies than he was a master of the art of poetry. This is not to say that he failed to carry out the procedures prescribed by Nash, nor that he was universally disliked. On the contrary he impressed many who, like Smollett's Lydia, were not hard to please:

As soon as we were settled in our lodgings, we were visited by the Master of Ceremonies; a pretty little gentleman, so sweet, so fine, so civil and polite, that in our country he might pass for the prince of Wales; then he talks so charmingly, both in verse and prose, that you would be delighted to hear him discourse, for you must know that he is a great writer, and has got five tragedies ready for the stage.

Smollett here does not try to conceal his contempt for the 'pretty little gentleman' with his absurd literary pretensions. He was insignificant in physical as well as in literary stature (after his death the *Bath Guide* referred to him as a 'diminutive apology for an M.C.'), and his authority was minimal. He was, for example, quite unable to quell the battle which on one occasion followed a quarrel between two ladies of quality in the ballroom, when 'caps, lappets, curls, cushions, diamond pins, and pearls strewed the floor of those rooms wherein during Nash's time order was supreme'. No wonder that for much of his time as Master of Ceremonies he had to cope as best he might with a determined campaign against him, led by Quin the actor. Apart from the fact that it was he who gave Herschel a place in the orchestra at the Rooms, his contribution to the life of the city was slight and ineffective.

Worse was to come. When Derrick died in 1769, a squabble broke out as to his successor. Each of the two Assembly Rooms had its own candidate and its own faction. There was a disgraceful scene at Simpson's rooms only a week after Derrick's death, when fighting broke out between the two parties, and the Mayor had to be hurriedly summoned to read the Riot Act. So low had Bath sunk within ten years of Nash's death.

Captain Wade, a nephew of the Field Marshal, and thus a cousin, on the sinister side, of Ralph Allen, was eventually chosen to succeed Derrick, and he managed, after a long period of increasing chaos and ill-feeling between the rival Assembly Rooms, to produce a programme acceptable to both. When, in 1777, he had to pay damages to the husband of a lady he had seduced, he was forced to resign and in his place two Masters of Ceremonies were appointed, one for each of the Rooms.

We need not concern ourselves with the later dynasty of Masters of Ceremonies, each one less significant than his predecessor. They stumbled on in the footsteps of Nash, but the task of maintaining proper social standards was beyond them. The rules forbidding the wearing of aprons, boots and spurs had constantly to be re-published, and dress regulations were made increasingly more detailed as the social status of the visitors sank and their ignorance of correct forms of dress grew. An extract from the rules published in 1777 for the New Rooms shows this:

that Ladies who intend to dance Minuets be dressed in a suit of Clothes, a full-trimm'd Sacque, or full-trimm'd Italian Night Gown and Petticoat, with Lappets and dressed Hoops.
N.B. Hoops of the smallest Size, commonly called Pocket-Hoops, are by no means proper to be worn with Lappets. . . . It is also expected, that no Lady will appear in an Apron of any Kind at the Monday's

57 Pump Room interior during a lull (J. C. Nattes, 1806)

Ball. That Gentlemen who dance Minuets do wear a full-trimm'd suit of Clothes or *French* Frock, Hair or Wig dressed with a Bag. All other Dresses of Fancy, with a Cape or Lappel, are not sufficient to attend on Ladies, who are obliged by the Rules of the Assembly to appear in full Dress.

The need to issue such precise instructions on matters with which polite society was fully familiar speaks for itself. It is no wonder

that the public balls and assemblies began to be shunned by the more fastidious visitors, who now preferred to entertain each other at the private parties which had been anathema to Nash. In 1780 Fanny Burney spent the season at Bath, staying with the Thrales at 14 South Parade, and took pains to avoid 'the showy, tonish people who are only to be seen by going to the Rooms, which we never do'. On Sundays, says Jane Austen, in

Northanger Abbey, there was 'not a genteel face to be seen' at the Pump Room.

The Rooms and Parades were still thronged, but no longer by the quality. The snobs, social climbers and *nouveaux riches* had taken over. Bath was becoming a caricature of itself, and London began to sneer and stay away.

To cater for a new and less discerning clientele strange forms of entertainment were sometimes provided. One such was at Bathwick Villa, the home of Alderman Ferry, the City Chamberlain, dismissed in 1780 owing to an unhappy failure to balance the books of the City Treasury. Fanny Burney visited the villa in the staid company of the Bishop of Peterborough. She found an ornate 'Gothick' house whose most interesting feature was the dining-room. By an ingenious mechanical device the dining-table was designed to rise through a trap-door in the floor. Miss Burney and the bishop watched this odd procedure and were startled by the descent from the ceiling of a carved eagle which took up in its beak the cloth covering the table, to reveal a rich display of cakes, sweetmeats and jellies. It is not clear whether the Alderman charged for admission to this spectacle, or whether it was shown only by invitation to respectable acquaintances. In 1783 the villa was bought by Marett, a wine-merchant, and opened to the general public as a place of entertainment. For a season's subscription of 2*s*. 6*d*. he provided a tea-garden, the use of newspapers, dinners, suppers and fireworks. For the convenience of patrons a ferry was run at the site of the present Cleveland Bridge.

It had always been a part of the social round of Bath to stroll in the gardens and on the promenades, where to be recognised and to be bowed to was a confirmation of one's acceptance by society. For this purpose it was an advantage for strolling to be concentrated into relatively confined spaces. In this way one saw and was seen by more people of the right sort than in more spacious areas. In London, Vauxhall and the recently opened Ranelagh had a different function. They offered outdoor entertainment to a large public. The fashionable world patronised them in a mood of condescension, finding amusement and a certain thrill in rubbing shoulders with the common people and avoiding the touts and pickpockets who were always present. The gardens were immensely popular. There was no equivalent of Ranelagh at Bath until Sydney Gardens, planned by Baldwin as a main feature of the development of the Pulteney Estate, was opened in 1795. It at once repeated the success of its metropolitan counterpart. Interest was added to the natural beauty of its tree-lined walks by artificial waterfalls, grottoes, a labyrinth, thatched pavilions and even a sham castle with cannon. Two iron bridges in the Chinese style were built over the canal which ran through the gardens. Nothing of all this remains except a charming rotunda at the far end of the gardens. The entertainment provided consisted of public breakfasts, bowling, outdoor concerts and above all, fireworks.

Since the gardens were popular with all classes it might be thought that they met Nash's objective of the free mingling of all levels of society; but this was not so. The patrons of the gardens did not mingle with each other. The entertainment provided was not social in Nash's sense. Nobility, gentry, servants and the new

58 The Kennet and Avon canal, Bath

59 Jane Austen's house, Sydney Place

urban labouring classes watched the fireworks or admired the waterfalls in their own separate groups. In any case when Nash spoke of all classes of society it did not occur to him to include those not of gentle birth. Sydney Gardens provided, in fact, an outdoor setting for individual entertainment and private parties. They represented the antithesis of Nash's social proposition.

This is the Bath of Jane Austen, observed on her visits as a young woman in the last years of the century. *Northanger Abbey*, whose scene is largely Bath, was written perhaps while she was staying with her Bath cousins, certainly in intervals between visits. Her sharp, ironic eye missed little, and she wrote while it was all fresh in her mind. *Persuasion*, the second of Jane Austen's novels, whose main scene is Bath, was written long after she had left the city for her native Hampshire. In this book, Sir William Elliott, a pompous snob, shrewdly chooses Bath as the ideal place in which to make his home. The very presence of large crowds of vulgar visitors lends him distinction by contrast and the absence of the top ranks of society gives him a position of eminence which he could not have held in London. Here he could be 'important at comparatively little expense', and his title, though a modest one, gave him the entrée to the best Bath society. 'The elegant stupidity of private parties' which provided the main evening amusement, suited him admirably. And there were many like him.

Bath now began to make an appeal not only to a new type of visitor but to attract a new sort of resident. Here was a city of fine streets and good houses, first-class concerts and plays, a fashionable tradition and an active social life, with a constant supply of new faces, some of which at least were respectable. If only one avoided the vulgarities and jostlings of the public rooms, particularly in the season, life could be very pleasant. And it was, as Sir William Elliott had found, cheap. It was thus an ideal place of retirement for those of limited means.

Already in 1783, Mrs Thrale, Dr Johnson's friend, had settled in Gay Street on the death of her husband. In the following year, in the face of universal disapproval, she married Gabriele Piozzi, a young Italian music teacher. After a short stay in Italy, she returned to England with him, spending the winters in Gay

Street, where she lived permanently after his death in 1809. Although now nearly 70, she continued to entertain with more energy than decorum. There were, we are told, 700 guests at her eightieth birthday party, who watched with astonishment as she led off the dancing with her newest protégé. She died in the following year. Her house, on the west side of Gay Street, is easily distinguishable from its neighbours by the richness of its ornament.

Parsons, generals and admirals all brought their small pensions to Bath, and lived out their last years in modesty and an atmosphere of gentility. Nelson, in the long intervals of half-pay between commissions, lived in a small house in Pierrepont Street. Admiral Arthur Phillip, whose convict settlement at Sydney led to the foundation of New South Wales and the development of Australia, retired to Bennett Street, where he died in 1814. In 1801, the Reverend George Austen retired to Bath, bringing his daughter Jane, with him; they lived in Sydney Place until his death four years later. Fanny Burney, now Madame d'Arblay, settled in Bath in 1815 with her husband, the émigré French general. 'Bath,' she said, 'is . . . the only town for us, since here, all the year round, there is always the town at command and always the country for prospect, exercise and delight.' She was only expressing a view widely held as the century advanced, and indeed still valid today.

As a fashionable resort, Bath's day was over, and the very name of the city became a byword for pretentious vulgarity. Dickens' description of Samuel Pickwick's visit in 1827 is a caricature of a caricature. Angelo Cyrus Bantam, Esq. M.C., 'a charming young man of not much more than fifty', with his scent, false teeth and obsequious manners, greeting Pickwick with his cry of 'Welcome to Ba-ath, sir', is not convincing as a King of Bath in the Nash tradition. Lady Snuphanuph, Lord Mutanhed and Mrs Colonel Wygsby are absurd snobs. Their background is provided by 'a vast number of queer old ladies and decrepit old gentlemen'. It is understandable that Sam Weller's reaction to his first sight of Bath was a mixture of polite indifference and sardonic amusement. The glory had indeed departed.

We will not follow the fading history of the city any further;

it is not the Bath we know. The streets, as splendid as ever, are no longer full of gaiety and noise. The inhabitants are older, and move slowly over the wide pavements. The decorum which it was Nash's concern to establish, and which his successors were not able to maintain, is now the normal pattern of life. It will degenerate into the graceless respectability of the Victorian Age.

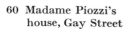

60 Madame Piozzi's house, Gay Street

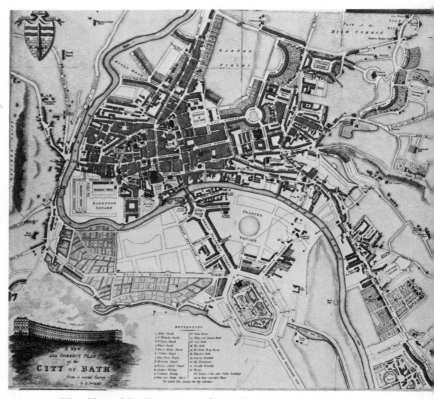

61 The City of Bath, c. 1810, from the survey by B. Donne

180

POSTSCRIPT

TODAY AND TOMORROW

Bath in the twentieth century presents a problem which it is easy enough to state. It is how to preserve what is worth preserving without condemning the city to the rôle of a museum. Modernisation and expansion must take place and communication with and within the city must be efficient: otherwise Bath dies. The streets of Bath were spaciously designed, but for sedan chairs and promenaders, not for heavy transport trucks and double-decker buses. Commerce requires new premises, often in or near the city centre, which must be functional but need not be beautiful. Some of the fine Georgian façades belong to flimsily-built structures near the end of their useful lives.

These are some of the data. There is no easy solution to the problem they set. To add to the difficulties, in late Victorian times and in the early years of this century a good deal of nasty but desperately durable building was permitted and fine eighteenth-century work destroyed. Modern shop-fronts in Milsom Street and Kingsmead Square, in all styles or in no style, insult the designs of Baldwin and Strahan. In the very heart of Nash's Bath the Empire Hotel, huge and execrable, leers over the Orange Grove and turns an ill-shapen shoulder on Pulteney Bridge (the bombs of the Luftwaffe missed this horrible building, but whether by bad aiming or deliberate malice is an open question).

There is no longer any danger, as far as one can see, that offensive new building will be allowed in the vicinity of the

Georgian city. The city authorities are fully alive to their responsibilities. The Bath Preservation Trust and other bodies keep a sharp eye on the situation. The danger is rather that fanatical preservationists will exert such effective pressure that no new building, however good, will be permitted. This was shown only a year or two ago, when a building of fine contemporary design was proposed to replace an undistinguished early nineteenth-century block in the Abbey Churchyard. The backwoodsmen of preservationism mobilised a massive opposition to it, got innocent celebrities to write letters to *The Times* and established an effective lobby in city circles. The enlightened lovers of Bath and of good building were overwhelmed. The building never got off the drawing-board.

The regulation that all new building must be faced in Bath stone or an approved imitation was an obvious one to impose and a relatively easy one to enforce. It succeeds in its purely negative aim of preventing the use of materials whose colour and texture are not in keeping with the rest of the city. It is not possible, however, to ensure by regulation that new building shall be beautiful, nor to prescribe the degree of originality permissible to the architect. A good deal of the building that has been permitted is to many eyes, including mine, intolerably inoffensive. One would like to see buildings whose style and character make a positive addition to the beauty of the city in the idiom of our own age. It is perhaps too much to expect. To many of those who are most concerned to protect Georgian Bath from architectural marauders, originality is only one form of vandalism.

A different problem is posed by the decay of Georgian buildings whose design is better than their internal structure. Shall their façades be restored while the buildings behind them are reconstructed on modern lines? Where restoration is considered to be impossible, as on the south side of Kingsmead Square, shall a faithful replica be made, or shall the new frontage be in modern style? There is no universally applicable solution. In each individual case the argument will be heated and decisions, even wrong decisions, hard to reach.

Inevitably later owners have introduced detailed changes in the frontages of Georgian buildings which mar the original design. One of the most widespread of these affects the windows. Originally these consisted of small panes of glass held in place by glazing-bars. Large panes of plate-glass have now generally been substituted. This apparently minor change has an extraordinary effect on the appearance of the façade as a whole. This can be well seen in Gay Street where Madame Piozzi's house has its glazing-bars while the neighbouring houses have lost theirs, or in the Circus where they have been restored in certain houses. It becomes clear that the glazing-bars made necessary in the first instance by the smallness of available glass-panes were used by the original architects as key-features of the design, giving scale and interest to the whole. Where they have been restored, not without controversy, the small cost has been amply repaid.

If a relatively small issue like the restoration of glazing-bars can lead to skirmishes, larger questions can cause open war. The bitterest battles are those which are fought when a needed improvement involves the demolition of buildings of architectural interest. The dilemma has sharp horns. In any ancient city problems exist, especially those which arise from the ever-increasing densities of traffic, which can be solved only by the widening of streets or the provision of new traffic-channels. The buildings which have to be demolished in such a process are generally old ones. As often as not they are beautiful as well. A city government responsible for the economic and social development of the community as well as for the preservation of the achievements of the past must in such situations make decisions for which it will be execrated by one faction or another. On one side are ranged the hard-faced 'realists' who insist that the past must at any cost yield to the demands of the present; on the other are the committed preservationists prepared to go to all lengths to prevent the destruction of any old building regardless of merit. In the din and confusion generated by the extremists, few perhaps in number but very vociferous, it is hard for the cool voice of reason to make itself heard. It is perhaps less remarkable that some of the decisions taken are bad than that any sane decisions are taken at all.

The greatest controversy of all, over the future development of the city as a whole, has lasted twenty-five years. An incredibly complex problem, it appears at last to be near solution, at least in its major outlines. Towards the end of the Second World War, Bath faced the task of repairing the damage caused by air-raids. This was clearly the moment to devise a plan for the future development of Bath, into which post-war reconstruction could be woven. Sir Patrick Abercrombie, the leading authority on town planning, was invited to undertake this work, in consultation with the city architect. The Abercrombie Report of 1945 was the result. It is an impressive document. It made bold and imaginative provision for new public buildings, including a civic centre, a much-needed concert hall and new accommodation for the Mineral Water Hospital in a large health centre. Nash himself would, one feels, have been pleased. The plan also offered a partial solution to the traffic problem, already serious. The bill for the implementation of the plan would, however, have been heavy, and perhaps for this reason the Report was not adopted.

Meanwhile a new threat, not only to Bath but to every city in the civilised world, had arisen and was to grow at a frightening rate. Year by year the weight and volume of motor traffic multiplied at a formidable pace. There is no reason to believe that it will not go on doing so. Car-control has now become as important as birth-control for the future of the human race and as difficult to impose.

To save Bath from destruction by the motor-car a ring-road by-passing the city might have provided a means, if it had been feasible. For Bath, however, clinging to the steep sides of the Avon valley and surrounded by hills, such a solution was clearly impracticable. All efforts to relieve the congestion in the centre of the city by opening up routes for through-traffic on its outskirts had largely failed: and every year the numbers and size of vehicles increased. Traffic from all directions converged and still converges implacably on Queen Square, choking all the roads leading to it and converting the square itself into a rush-hour Piccadilly, with the difference that the rush-hour lasts all day. The other main roads in the city centre, all of them the work of the great Georgian architects, suffer similarly.

Sir Colin Buchanan, the acknowledged expert on the traffic problems of cities, was then commissioned to make a study of

Bath and to make proposals for its redevelopment with particular reference to its communications. The Buchanan Report (as it is generally called) of 1968 is a work of understanding technical expertise and vision. Its key proposal, the provision of an east-west relief road carried under the heart of the city by a tunnel, met with fierce opposition, mainly on the grounds of cost. Predictably, amateur town-planners innocent of technical knowledge produced chimerical alternatives. More serious suggestions designed to save money were also examined. None was seen to provide a solution, and finally, to the credit of both city and national authorities, Buchanan's plan was formally accepted. It was, however, never implemented and must now be regarded as a dead letter. It might have saved the city. It is certain that no scheme less radical will do so and none has since been devised.

The future is not all gloom, however. While Abercrombie and Buchanan have been relegated to dusty shelves in the city archives, new life has sprung up elsewhere.

In 1966 a University was established on the heights of Claverton Down on the south-eastern outskirts of the city. A finer site for a university could not easily be imagined. Nor is any city in England more proper to be the home of an institution of learning than Bath, with its unique cultural background.

In its twenty years of life the University has revived, with a difference, a city Nash would have recognised and approved, where a permanent but ever-changing population of students creates the bustle and gaiety absent in the years when Bath was little more than a place of retirement for the elderly. Now too, tourists in mounting numbers throng its streets and splendid crescents, crowd into the Pump Room and the Assembly Rooms, admire the Abbey and wonder at the Roman Baths. Bath will live. It has its unique place in the social and architectural history of Britain, a present that lives up to its past and a future with all the ingredients of greatness. Only let it never become a museum: conservation must go hand in hand with the imaginative innovation our times demand.

APPENDIX

THE GUILDHALL PORTRAITS

(*Victoria Art Gallery and City Collections*)

The following is a selection of portraits which may be seen in the Guildhall, Bath.

SUBJECT	ARTIST
Banqueting Room	
Ralph Allen	William Hoare
Christopher Anstey	William Hoare
William Pitt, Earl of Chatham	William Hoare
Lieutenant-General Wade	J. B. van Diest
Frederick Prince of Wales (son of George II)	Jeremiah Davidson
Augusta Princess of Wales (wife of the foregoing)	Jeremiah Davidson
George III	Studio of Reynolds
Queen Charlotte (wife of George III)	Studio of Reynolds
Committee Room No. 1	
George I	after Kneller
George III	Studio of Allan Ramsay
Queen Charlotte	Studio of Allan Ramsay
Henry VII	Jan Gossart
Henry VIII	after Holbein
James I	unknown

186

Committee Room No. 2
John Churchill, Duke of Marlborough   Pieter van der Werff
Sarah, Duchess of Marlborough   Pieter van der Werff
Mary of Modena (2nd wife of James II)   Willem Wissing

Committee Room No. 3
Dr Samuel Johnson   John Opie
Richard Nash   William Hoare
Samuel Richardson (the novelist)   William Hoare
John Palmer (lessee of the Theatre Royal,   William Hoare
    Bath)
William Hoare, RA   self-portrait

Committee Room No. 4
Thomas Barker   self-portrait
Charles Dickens   unknown
William Linley (youngest son of   Studio of
    Thomas Linley)   Sir Thomas Lawrence
'Beau' Nash   after William Hoare
    by Mary Hoare

Mayor's Parlour
Mrs Christopher Anstey   William Hoare
Richard Nash   Adrien Carpentiers

Corridors and Hall
Thomas Barker and Charles Spackman   Thomas Barker
William Dawson, Master of Ceremonies   Thomas Hickey
Richard Nash   Thomas Worlidge
Alexander Pope   Edward Wright
Major Simpson (the last Master of   Edwin Swan
    Ceremonies)

SELECT BIBLIOGRAPHY

Barbeau, A., *Life and Letters at Bath in the Eighteenth Century*, 1904.
Ison, Walter, *The Georgian Buildings of Bath*, London 1948; Kingsmead
    Reprints 1969.
    These two delightful and scholarly books are indispensable for any
    modern writer about Bath. I happily acknowledge my debt to them.

The following list is a selection of works which have been of particular
value to me and may be of interest to other students.
Abercrombie, Sir Patrick, Owens, J. and Mealand, H. A., *A Plan for Bath*
    (the Abercrombie Report), London 1945.
Anstey, Christopher, *The New Bath Guide*, 1766. (Reprinted 1970 Adams
    & Dart.)
Buchanan, Professor Colin, *Bath, A Study in Conservation* (the Buchanan
    Report), HMSO 1968.
Colby, R., *Mayfair: A Town Within London*, Country Life 1966.
Cunliffe, Barry, 'The Temple of Sulis Minerva at Bath', reprinted from
    Antiquity XL, 1966.
Davis, C. E., *The Mineral Baths of Bath*, Bath 1883.
Falconer, Randle W. and Brabazon, Beaufort, *The Royal Mineral Water
    Hospital, Bath*, Bath 1888.
Freeman, H. W., *The Thermal Baths of Bath*, Bath 1888.
Goldsmith, Oliver, *The Life of Richard Nash, Esquire*, London 1762.
Gosse, Philip, *Dr Viper (Biography of Philip Thicknesse)*, London 1952.
Guidott, Thomas, *Lives and Characters of the Physicians of Bath*, 1676.
James, P. Rowland, *The Baths of Bath in the 16th and early 17th Centuries*,
    Arrowsmith 1938.
Leland, John, *The Itinerary of 1535–1543* (ed. Lucy Toulmin Smith),
    London 1907.
Sitwell, Edith, *Bath*, London 1932.
Symons, Katharine, *The Grammar School of King Edward VI, Bath*,
    Bath 1930.
Taylor, A. J., *The Roman Baths of Bath* (revised by Sir Mortimer Wheeler
    and B. H. St J. O'Neil), Bath 1951.
Thicknesse, Philip, *The New Prose Bath Guide*, Bath 1778.
Tyte, William, *Bath in the Eighteenth Century*, Bath 1903.
Warner, Richard, *History of Bath*, 1801.
Wood, John, *An Essay Towards a Description of Bath*, 1749 (Kingsmead
    Reprint 1969).
Anonymous, *Characters at the Hot Well at Bristol in September and at Bath
    in October* 1723.
The Bath Guide (published at Bath annually from 1742, for the use of
    visitors).

INDEX

Figures in bold type refer to illustrations

Index